HORSEPOWER

HORSEPOWER
A Memoir

Annette Israel

iUniverse, Inc.
New York   Bloomington

iUniverse Star
an iUniverse, Inc. imprint

iUniverse books may be ordered through booksellers or by contacting:

iUniverse
1663 Liberty Drive
Bloomington, IN 47403
www.iuniverse.com
1-800-Authors (1-800-288-4677)

ISBN: 978-1-4401-0251-6 (sc)
ISBN: 978-1-4401-0254-7 (ebook)

Printed in the United States of America

iUniverse rev. date: 11/25/2008

For God
From whom all good things come
And to whom all good things go.

ACKNOWLEDGMENTS

THIS STORY IS TRUE. Some names have been changed to protect the privacy of certain individuals.

For my parents, who helped me find my talents and pointed me in the right direction to find the tools I'd need along the way, thank you.

Thanks to Megan Crawford for her expertise in catching all of the initial typos and punctuation errors in this manuscript.

Thanks to Gary Lane who talked me through formatting changes on the phone while he was in Virginia, and to Nick Bagalay for coming to my home and actually *doing* the additional formatting changes.

Thanks to Jeanne Rouston at Kopy Korner for scanning photos and uploading the whole package to the publisher. For all of you who helped me with the computer issues, I appreciate everything. I couldn't have done it without you. Thanks to Jim Binder at Isabella Bank & Trust.

Thanks to Mark, Stephen, Zach, Shawn, Shelley, Lynn, Jan, Diane, and all of the folks at iUniverse. Thank you, Mark Mandell.

Kathy—best friend and horse bud—thank you for always being there for nearly four decades, during joyful and painfully rough times. Remember "Rocky Top," the pie, the pizza, and all of the horse shows all over the country? Always remember the laughs and tears we've shared. You've never once hurled darts at my dreams or the risks I've taken.

Nancy—best friend and horse bud—I've never once heard you speak the words, "If you need anything, let me know." Without exception, you *always* set aside whatever is going on in your life—and go. You have also been there through need, grief, and happiness. We speak the language of the horse and we understand. You alone were the person who stood just behind me, but within earshot, cheering this book on to completion. Remember that this project began on an old computer you loaned to me. "At least it will get you started," you said. If the dictionary contained photographs and someone looked up the definition of "best friend," they'd find your picture there.

Thanks to, and a special remembrance for Charles Ritter, who passed away before the completion of this book.

CHAPTER
One

SCRATCHES AND SCARS DEEPLY etch the rugged black leather of the old horse collar. The metal buckles are pitted and brown with rust. On the inside, the leather is textured and feels like sandpaper, corroded with layers of historical horse sweat.

Outside my kitchen window, beneath the silvery blue dusk of winter, snow is billowing in great gusts across the now barren hayfield. Prompted by memories, and urged on by the weight of the old collar as it rests heavily against my knee, I am eased into telling a story that began with a question I asked my father when I was sixteen years old.

"Can I please have a Belgian?"

"You already have a horse," he said. "What are you going to do with a draft horse?"

"Ride it," I said, my brown eyes peering hopefully into my father's face.

I'd found an ad in the paper describing a yearling Belgian colt, and buying him seemed wonderfully logical to my adolescent mind.

"Someday, when you are an adult, and you want a draft horse, you can have one," Papa said, and that was the end of that conversation.

My father had grown up on a farm in Michigan's Upper Peninsula where draft horses were used for pulling logs out of the woods and hauling hay. They weren't riding horses. Farmers had a deep respect for the power of these massive creatures, but they never thought of them as pets. They were working animals, and they worked hard.

As a child, I often sat on my father's lap and said, "Tell me about when you were little." That was the only cue he needed to launch into tales of the two workhorses his father owned. One was named Queenie and the other named Babe. Babe was an older, white Percheron mare. She was a dependable workhorse and threw her weight into the collar, pulling her share and more when the team was hitched to a load. Queenie was a younger, bay draft mare that should have won an Academy Award. Queenie would make all of the appropriate huffs and puffs like she was straining and working hard when she was hitched. In reality, though, she was only pretending, forcing Babe to do all of the work. When my father slowed the team, Babe would appropriately stop pulling, but Queenie was always caught red-hoofed. Since she'd been acting all along, she didn't realize they'd been asked to stop, and so she would continue her stage-worthy performance. I sat wide-eyed in wonder at the stories and descriptions of those great horses. Papa often said that Babe was durable and of sound mind and strong character. "She was wise and kind," he said. Queenie possessed a dark mahogany beauty and large expressive eyes, but that was about the extent of her attributes. I knew that my father loved both mares, but for different reasons. He was able to forgive Queenie for all her misdeeds the moment she transgressed. Beauty expects, and receives, softness. I am confident that this man, who never once spanked me, never struck a horse either.

It's been said that we are born with the love of horses. It's not something that we can quickly or eloquently put into words. You either have it, or you don't. Such a deep inborn passion is not something you chase after; rather, it finds you, fills you, and becomes you. It never goes away. My mother told me stories of how I sat in my highchair as a baby, entranced by a little blue rocking horse rattle that she had put on my tray. No other toy held my interest. Later, at a year and a half old, I often stood in the living room captivated by our black-and-white television set—but just at certain times. Mama figured out that I did this only when a cowboy named Vint Bonner was galloping his horse across the screen.

At the grand old age of four years, I received a real rocking horse for Christmas. I rode my horse every day, all day long, rocking and bouncing on its squeaky springs in time to music from my mom's record collection. Daily, my mother had to lift me off of my dapper steed when I had fallen fast asleep.

Horsepower

For most of my early childhood, I crawled around on all fours with soup cans attached to my hands so that they would sound like hooves. I stuffed one of my mother's scarves into the back of my pants for a tail. Sometimes I would put a pencil in my mouth for a bit and rig up shoelaces to resemble a bridle. I whinnied and snorted and practiced every noise a horse made. I even crawled down the sidewalk like this, oblivious to the fact that we had neighbors. Undoubtedly, as they peeked out their windows, they must have commented among themselves, "Eric and Adele sure have a strange little kid." Trips in the family car were adventures for me as my sharp, horse-crazed eyes steadfastly scanned out the windows in the hopes of spotting horses. Countless times, my father carried me on his shoulders up to some strange farmer's door to ask if his daughter could pet the horses over the fence. If my parents weren't watching, they'd find me off in the distance slogging through mud or knee-deep snow in order to get close to a horse. I collected horse statues, pictures, and anything and everything one might possibly need for horse ownership. I wrote pages of names for horses. I drew horses. I dreamed of horses. I lived and breathed horses.

When I turned ten, my parents started taking me to a local riding stable for a one-hour ride on a horse. The week in between each chance to be with a horse was painfully long and almost unbearable. I spent the weekdays daydreaming about horses, waiting anxiously for Saturday to roll around again. Once home after these rides, I would conveniently forget to wash the glorious scent of horse off of my hands for as long as I could avoid it. I would close my eyes, cup my hands over my nose, and breathe in the sweet, husky smell over and over. I'd finally have to give in when my mom persisted, "Did you wash your hands?" My love of horses was much more than a passing childhood fancy—it was an ache.

When I was twelve, I said a special novena to St. Joseph. A novena is said for nine consecutive mornings for anything you may desire. I asked for a horse before I reached my thirteenth birthday. On December 5, 1968, my parents bought me Velvet, a spirited, part-Arabian bay mare. The next day I turned thirteen. My parents never knew about the novena.

Life began for me when Velvet came. The touch and warmth of a horse had finally filled the shell that was supposed to be me. Velvet became the pulse that drove my life, and I had the freedom and time of youth to leisurely enjoy each moment with her.

I grew up in the city of Pontiac, Michigan, during a time that was both a challenge and a blessing, as each day continually dealt pages of yet-to-be-written history books. I walked hand in hand with my parents to the high school one day where we stood in a long line waiting to get our sugar cubes with little pink dots on them. I was only a toddler, but I remember the experience even though I couldn't comprehend the significance that the little pink dot held for the entire world. Polio had never touched my family—and never would.

My first experience with death occurred on one fall day in 1963. I came home from school and, instead of bounding through the door as usual, I felt the occasion was important enough to ring the doorbell. My mom answered the door with a slightly perplexed look on her face.

"Mamma," I said, "President Kennedy is dead."

My mother dropped to her knees and said, "Honey, don't ever joke about something like that."

I saw something wash over her that worried me. It had just slammed into her that her second grader was home at an odd time, and it was improbable that she would concoct such a tale. She left me standing in the doorway. I watched as she bolted through the house and collapsed in front of the radio. Slowly, I walked into the house and stood near her as her sobs became nearly deafening. It was as if I wasn't there at all—as if I'd ceased to exist—and I was scared. It was the first time I'd ever felt truly alone. It was the first time that I realized my mother was a separate being with feelings of her own, and that she didn't exist solely to serve my every need. It was the first time I saw her cry.

We watched our black-and-white television for days after the assassination. The "Six White Horses," the beautiful rider-less horse with the boots carried backwards. I thought, *How can anything I love so much be a part of something so sad?* But, we got through it and we went ahead with our lives.

A time of sharp contrasts, it was the age of LSD, hip-hugger jeans, and tie-dyed shirts, the Vietnam War, gas masks, and flowers propped into the barrels of rifles by college students. Protests and demonstrations seemed endless. Everyone had something to say.

One day I went to the high school to hear a young man speak. There were only a handful of us gathered in the auditorium even though he'd drawn national attention. Some people listened to his words; most dismissed him as a heretic. His name was Ralph Nader and his mission, on that day, was to forewarn us of the dangers of pollution—that we must change our output or we wouldn't have a planet.

Women began to challenge and they dared to dream that one day a little girl might grow up to become president. An American walked on the moon. Black people also dared to question and demand a fair share of dreams and the possibility of actually achieving them. And racial tension raged like one hot, continuous August day.

I attended Pontiac Central High School. It was a good school—not void of problems, but the only school I knew. I saw a student knifed in the hallway right in front of me. She survived the attack and graduated that year. Desks were often hurled out of windows, and fights broke out almost on a daily basis. I've always thought it so strikingly odd when I hear folks say that the heavy racism of the '60s and '70s occurred only in the South. So it is with any inhumane action people have eagerly joined in, until those who are wiser and more compassionate shake that turf, forcing us to see truth. Once our deeds are exposed, it's always someone else who did it, some other group that is responsible—it happened "over there." Ten brand-new school buses were torched and burned beyond recognition in Pontiac, Michigan. *White* parents did this in protest of black children being bussed to the schools their children attended. But new busses rolled into history anyway.

National Guardsmen lined up and down our street in full riot gear. I walked past them every morning on my way to school and at the close of each day. Tanks groaned their way through downtown, and every night the streets tried to sleep under the curfew.

1968 was bittersweet. My beloved Velvet, the answer to my prayers and dreams came into my life. It was also the year that Dr. Martin Luther King and Bobby Kennedy were assassinated. It was a tumultuous time; of that there can be no doubt. The pressure of those days and events were softened for me because I had a horse. I lived in the city and attended a tough city school. But, even though at times the whole world was rocketing off its foundation all around me, I was able to leave it every night after school and on the weekends when my mom or dad drove me out to the barn where Velvet was stabled.

As many youngsters do when they have a horse, I joined 4-H. Over the years, I competed in countless horse shows, even in the wintertime. I can still see my father's face turned up toward me as he bent over, chipping rock-like ice off of the trailer hitch. His soft hazel eyes blinked at the snow and sleet biting his cheeks.

"Do you really want to go?" he asked.

"Yes," I said.

On horse show mornings, I was the one who rang in the day. It was easy to do because I was always so excited about going to a show that I stayed up the whole night in anticipation. Early in the morning, I would tiptoe into my parents' bedroom in the dark and gently touch Papa on the shoulder. "It's time to go," I'd whisper.

He always took a deep, regretful breath. "Annette, it's three-thirty in the morning," he'd say.

"I know, but I have to work Velvet."

While I was busy scurrying around, getting last minute tack loaded into the truck, my father made our usual breakfast of Cream of Wheat cereal with toast and peanut butter. We put the Cream of Wheat *on* the toast with peanut butter and ate it as our own special invention. And we had hot cocoa made with milk. Those mornings are carved into my past, but they mean more to me now than they did at the time, and are safely tucked away in my collection of special memories.

We loaded up and drove to various locations and fairgrounds throughout the state to participate in shows. Velvet was a feisty mare. She pranced and jigged sideways every time I rode her, and she needed a lot of exercise before she was calm enough to enter the show ring. I always insisted on getting to the show grounds early so that I could work her. Many times, when we pulled into a deserted lot, my father would look around and say quietly, as if to no one in particular, "We're the only ones here." His accurate observation didn't diminish my utter joy. It didn't matter to me that it was still dark, and I never seemed to notice that there would be just one lone rider in the warm-up ring for hours—me. I happily got my horse ready and rode her.

Dad and I were tired and dusty when we returned home at the end of a long day, but it was what we did, and it was fun. Mom and I had a routine we followed after every show. It began when I won my first ribbon and placed a pink, fifth-place rosette into her open palms.

"How did you do?" she would ask.

"Close your eyes and open your hands," I'd say.

In the early days, there might have been just a solitary ribbon, the color denoting a low placing. But, over the years, there were many trophies and blue ribbons that I placed in her hands. Velvet and I even qualified for the state 4-H show several times in my last years as a 4-H member. Mom never cared what color the ribbons were or how many I won. She didn't care if there weren't any at all; she only wanted me to have fun.

Mamma didn't go to the shows very often, but she made nearly all of my show outfits. At first my costumes looked homemade and downright silly because we didn't know the styles. I once sewed bright red pompons and tassels all over Velvet's western saddle pad and hung them from her bridle. I was the only kid at the shows that summer decked out so colorfully and so noticeably. Slowly, I converted into a more stylishly attired horsewoman. Mom made many show clothes that complemented both the horse and me, and I refrained from decorating them so profusely.

I did find an appropriate place for all of those tassels, however, when I saw my first Arabian native costume class at a show. *All* of the horses and their riders were wearing beautiful, handmade costumes literally covered in tassels. So, one summer, my mom and I worked side by side for weeks sewing blue tassels and silvery beads, sequins, and jewels onto a creation that she had made for both Velvet and me. For years, the costume won many blue ribbons.

When I turned seventeen, my father decided to teach me how to hook up and pull the horse trailer by myself. I was already a good driver, and Papa trusted me out on the road. He was also envisioning retirement from pulling a horse trailer to every horse show in the state of Michigan on every Saturday and Sunday every weekend of the year for the next twenty years of his life.

"It's time you learned to pull the trailer," he said.

I wanted to learn. It meant freedom and signaled a formal step toward adulthood. I was so excited that I couldn't sleep for several nights as I watched visions passing through my mind. I saw myself hauling six horses at a time in a grandiose trailer to California by myself within the next year, and returning home with a truckload of trophies. In my dreams I'd manage to project beyond the fact that we only had a homemade, one-horse trailer with plywood sides.

On the day my training was to start, Pops and I went to the backyard. He tossed me the keys to his faded green Chevrolet truck.

"First, we have to hook up the trailer," he said. "Just back the truck up to the trailer."

"Okay," I chirped, and gingerly performed the task.

I jumped out of the truck and strutted to the hitch. Papa was waiting for me. His eyes slowly fell to the hitch, dragging my eyes down with his.

"It takes practice," he said.

I glared at the hitch. It was about one foot shy of the coupler and about eighteen inches off to the side.

"You can't just back up more now; you have to pull forward and realign the truck and then back again," he said.

My father gave me pointers on backing straight, but it sure took practice. I was able to ace backing straight; it was the precise distance to make the connection that stumped me. It was tedious and frustrating. I'd back the truck up, jump out and check how I'd done, then get in the truck again and back up more only to find that I'd gone too far. My face would feel hot and flushed. Sometimes it took as many as fifteen attempts before I got it right. Through it all, my father waited patiently. He could have gone into the house, but he didn't. He didn't say anything either. He just let me work through the problem. Sometimes, when I cranked the hitch down, the weight of the trailer balanced heavily just on the edge, like the pointer of a prize wheel wavering between five dollars and five thousand dollars. I'd wait breathlessly, and then the hitch would slide down onto the ball with a pleasing "clunk." Sometimes, all I'd have to do was tap the hitch or the trailer with my toe and the hitch would plop down onto the ball.

Once I was able to hook up the trailer within a few minutes, it was time to take the rig out onto the road. Pulling a trailer is a whole new aspect of driving. You can feel it resisting the truck and surging against it, awkwardly stuck to you like a cumbersome cast on a broken leg. My father continually explained things as we chugged along.

"Watch the curb ... watch the curb, now, when you go around a corner."

The truck had a manual transmission, so I had to learn to ease the clutch out with just the right pressure on the gas pedal. These were things I had previously mastered, but grasping the feel of the right balance with the *trailer* was like learning to drive a stick shift all over again.

"Remember, when the trailer is loaded, you have a living thing back there. You have to think of the horse," Papa said.

It occurred to me then that, when he pulled my horse, we glided to stops and eased forward so smoothly that Velvet never had to take a step to catch her balance. You never knew a horse was behind you; there was only silence in the trailer. My father explained how he took the corners, "Slow and easy, so you don't upset the horse."

During one of our last driving lessons, my father drove. He pulled the truck into the local high school driver education range, which was deserted that day because it was a Sunday. There, he taught me how to back the trailer with finesse. I learned very quickly that, when backing, a trailer thinks on its own, connives, and cunningly refuses to go in the direction in which you aim. It takes a lot of practice and a lot of skill because you must back the truck in the opposite direction that you want the trailer to go.

"Remember that Salty Badger Farms show and the mud?" Papa asked.

I did remember, and, at that moment, was greatly impressed. We had attempted to go to a show one Saturday in early March. It had been a typical Michigan winter with lots of snow. Great mounds of the stuff, piled on the sides of the roads, were melting in teasing splashes of sunshine that no longer belonged to winter, yet were not fully owned by spring. My father pulled down a dirt road and made it to the next turn only to find a sign telling us that the roads were closed because of the mud. There was nowhere to turn around. He had to back the trailer up for over a mile to make it back to the paved road. Sometimes it takes half a lifetime to appreciate such skill.

"What if you end up in the same situation?" he asked.

He taught me to back the trailer in straight lines, in curved lines, and for the entire length of the driving range. He taught me to back in all directions, and, within a few weeks, I felt like I could have backed us all the way to Mexico.

"There is something else we need to work on," he said one day, in his best attempt to be stern. He also said that he wanted to drive. I slowly got out of the truck and sat in the passenger seat. A familiar, wretched twinge stabbed me in the stomach. I knew what he meant.

"No, not the ramp," I said, and fashioned a perfect, foolproof pout.

"Gotta do it if you're going to go to your own horse shows," he said as he drove the truck straight toward the ramp.

"I'm not doing it. I don't know how to do it. I'll never know how to do it," I sputtered. "Why do you make me do this?"

There was no reply.

"The ramp" had always been a foreboding mountain looming constantly in my driving fears. At the high school driving range, there was a paved ramp, put in place for students just like me who had to learn to get a vehicle with a stick shift traveling up hill from a standstill—on the hill. My father taught me how to drive the truck up the slope, and he taught me how to get moving from a stop. He would drive the truck halfway up the ramp, shut it off and then change places with me.

With the trailer stuck to the truck, it was no different. He drove partially up and shut the engine off.

"Your turn," he announced.

Quivering, and almost turning on my well-practiced tears, I rolled myself out of the truck like slow molasses on a cold winter morning. I changed places with him.

"They make automatic shifters, you know," I said over my shoulder, giving my upturned lower lip one more chance.

"Automatic transmissions," he corrected. "Yes, but we don't have one. This is part of the deal, Annettska."

Papa sat in the passenger seat reading his newspaper, comfortably settled in for the duration. He whistled. My father always whistled, but he never once whistled a recognizable tune. There was no melody; it was just his personal jingle that always sounded the same. On that day, his whistling conveyed a message that, if we were going to get home that evening, I'd have to garner the concept and the feel of the right amount of gas and clutch to get the truck *and* trailer going up the hill smoothly instead of rolling backwards or stalling.

Learning to drive a stick shift is one of those milestones in your life that, once mastered, slides away and finds a permanent place to rest somewhere in the days gone by. You never think again about what an overwhelming challenge it was at the time because there is no need.

Amid the turmoil of my generation, I managed to make it through adolescence safely and drug free. I had something else to do, and the core of my universe was Velvet. Once, I heard my Uncle Karl comment that I'd lose interest in horses. He taunted, "Just wait until the boys come along, or a car. She'll leave those horses."

"Not my kid," my father said.

CHAPTER
Two

ADOLESCENCE HAS A WAY of tiptoeing into adulthood as methodically and as without pomp as dawn finds its sunlight. Suddenly, you notice it's daytime, and, just as suddenly, you notice that you aren't a little kid anymore.

Adulthood is a complete package. In that package there are age-appropriate trials and experiences, ripe and waiting. Sometimes you get to reach in that box and pluck one you think you'd like to try. Other times, it seems as if they are hurled at you when you are least prepared. When I was eighteen, my parents divorced after thirty-eight years of marriage. There were never issues of infidelity, alcohol, or drugs. My mom simply didn't want to be married to my dad anymore. Both of them had come from very poor families, and, on top of that, my mom was one of ten children. She also experienced pronounced mood swings, and, when the down times hit, she targeted my father. She was incredibly healthy otherwise, and I never knew her to be sick a day in her life. She never went to see a doctor except when babies were born. Back then, there weren't many resources for someone with depression, anxiety, or whatever mood disorder she might have had. Now, we have a vast arsenal of medications and counselors that are easy to find and within reach.

The divorce should never have happened. My father pleaded, offered to go to a marriage counselor, and then went to a marriage counselor on his own. None of that worked. My mom left and moved back to the Upper Peninsula. The day she left, she hugged me and walked out the front door leaving me standing in the living room. There was no choice for me—my whole world existed in the home I'd always known. My friends were there. My horse was there. It could have been a time of devastation, but I had this living, breathing creature that depended on me, loved me, and accepted me. Most important of all, Velvet listened.

I loved my mom. She was my best friend. Every day when I came home from school she was there. I'd go into her sewing room where she would be sewing or working on an oil painting, perch myself on a stool, and chat with her for hours. She was my favorite person to go shopping with, my best buddy to watch a movie with. Almost every night we'd sit together and watch *I Love Lucy* reruns, laugh like silly kids, and eat popcorn sprinkled with Parmesan cheese. I don't know why, but I didn't hate her when she left. Somewhere deep inside of me I'd found a fragment of acceptance that was enough to carry me through. A few times a year, I made the trip north to see her, although the distance made those visits difficult. We talked on the phone every day.

I grew up, earned an associates degree, and had a career as a state trooper, but horses were still the center of my world. I became a horse show judge, owned a breeding stallion that stood at public stud, and I raised foals and sold them. I had many beautiful champions. I also rescued abused and neglected horses. The work was hard and the hours long, but there was immeasurable joy in being able to do what I loved most.

When I was twenty-five, my mother was in a car accident and died three days after. Then my father died of cancer a year and a half later. Parents chisel out a piece of your heart and a piece of your soul, and they take those with them when they go, leaving behind a gaping void that only they had been able to fill. I was twenty-six years old and both were gone. I still needed my mom and dad and wanted them in my life. Even through the intense grief and longing, I was unable to see the sacrifices they had made for me—until now. Perhaps the grand prize for getting older is the gift of wisdom and the ability to reflect unselfishly. My folks were not perfect people, but they did the best they could with what they had to work with at the time.

My mom and my dad each had their trials and heartaches. My dad's mom committed suicide when my father was six years old. He was the one who found her. I have an older brother. His name was Wren Charles. I never knew him because he died shortly after birth. My parents never shared their sadness with me. I learned of these things late in life. Had I known from the time I was a child, how would it have changed me? I believe my parents chose to shoulder their pain alone rather than burden me with it, knowing that making it through childhood and surviving adolescence was burden enough.

They had given me my love of horses, but, more importantly, they had allowed it to grow and flourish. Now, it stings to remember every winter morning and the horse shows, every stitch—by hand—that went into that Arabian costume, the hours they put in, and the sacrifices they must have made to give me my dream, while their own dreams slid aside forever. It stings now because of my own childhood selfishness and it stings for monumental gratitude and the pain of its silence.

I don't think we actually know our parents while we are young. We have the absolute expectation that they exist for us. Do we ever truly learn about *their* dreams and aspirations? If they do give us hints, does it really matter to us when we are kids? My mom told me that, when she was a little girl, her dream was to dance. She said that she once found a torn ballet slipper in a garbage can. It was pink with satin ribbons. She told me how she sat on the sidewalk and jammed her foot into that slipper even though it was several sizes too small. She was elated that she was finally going to be a ballerina. She danced and she danced in that one ballet slipper on a blistered and bleeding foot until the slipper hung in dirty strings and would no longer lace up. With nine siblings, there was no money to pay for dance lessons. Years later, my mom would put on her records and the two of us would dance in the living room. We did this several times a week throughout my childhood and adolescence.

My father had horses, but not for pleasure. He told me that what he wanted the most in the whole wide world when he was a little boy was a bicycle. One day, he too found someone else's discarded junk—mere pieces of his dream. The wheels were all wobbly and the tires flat. The handlebars were bent and the pedals didn't go round. So, he took his bike to the top of a hill and launched himself down the grassy knoll. "Just once," my dad laughed, "and it broke to bits. But I got to ride that bike." There was no money for bicycles in his family. He often said that he was elated at Christmas if he received, "A shiny apple or a nice round orange." A bicycle never appeared under his Christmas tree.

I had a tricycle that I named Flicka, an orange bike with big fat tires and training wheels that I named Fury, a royal blue bike, a purple bike with silvery streamers flowing out of the handlebars, and a green bike with a basket. I remember the Sunday evenings in the summer when Papa would say, "Let's go for a bike ride." Now, as I look back, I understand the grin on his face that I saw every time I'd look over my shoulder at him slowly pedaling along, not in any specific direction of his own, just following me.

They were gone. Yet, I never felt completely separated from them because they'd been such a significant part of my horse world, and the horses remained a constant in my life.

For me, having a horse has never been just about being able to ride. It's much more than that. It's the scent of a horse, the touch of a horse, and the feel of vibrant life beneath your palms as your hands glide over a horse's silken coat. It's about a horse's warm breath steaming up into your face when he's munching grain on an early winter morning and smells like sweet cereal. It's about sharing in the history of a world that was carried forward by the power of horses—a history immersed in toil, hardship, danger, and companionship. It isn't just about riding; it's about the mystical, spiritual, and romantic relationship with a creature both fragile and powerful. It's about communication that transcends mere animal-human coexistence. It's a love story that began the moment man and horse first stood facing each other on some deserted, windswept plain so many thousands of years before us.

That same ancient wind carried me right from the beginning into the world of Arabian horses. With their beautifully sculpted, dished faces, large eyes, and lofty tail carriage, they are an artist's dream. They are brilliant, showy animals, both challenging and a joy to work with.

Preoccupied with my Arabians, I hadn't thought much about Belgians since I was a kid. But one day, while out getting a load of horse feed, I took a different road back from the mill. In the distance, I saw a farmer plowing his field with a team of the huge, copper-colored horses. The sun convinced me to pull my truck onto the shoulder of the road, get out, and watch. Goose bumps crept over my skin, and something deep inside of me began to stir. Was it the unconscious memory of a little blue horse rattle trying to surface, or visions of a white Percheron mare named Babe and a bay named Queenie? I stood there blinking away the tears in my eyes, my heart beating rapidly and tight against my chest as I watched the team of four forcing the earth to yield under their power. The fire in my heart for draft horses hadn't diminished over the years. It was still smoldering, just waiting to surge. I wanted to stay and watch the entire field fashioned into neat, brown furrows, but I had a schedule to keep, horses to work, and chores to do. I drove away from the Belgians and back into my own world. But that world was about to change drastically.

I began having strange feelings that God was moving strongly in my life, urging me to do something. The feeling intensified until I had no doubt I was to enter a life of service to God. My response was to walk away from everything I knew and did. I quit my job as a state trooper and found homes for all of my beloved horses. I became homeless in a matter of days. I lost my vehicle, all of my belongings, and gave everything away. I had no place to live and no where to go.

I learned about a woman who had an adult foster care home and needed a live-in aide. I'd receive no pay, but I'd have a room and food if I went there. For four years I lived and worked in that home, surviving on basically faith alone. I prayed continually and studied the Bible fourteen times through. I had nothing. I had to collect pop bottles to purchase one stamp; yet, every day I experienced miracles and I got to know God intimately and as a wise old friend with an incredible sense of humor. One day, I asked the Lord for one hundred dollars. Some type of promotional letter arrived that day, and, nestled in the advertising brochures, was a one-hundred-dollar bill but it was a fake, like the ones in Monopoly. I could almost hear the Lord saying, "But you didn't say a *real* hundred-dollar bill." I had nothing, yet I truly had everything that I needed. There were no frills, but all of my basic needs were met every single day. I never would have believed that I could change a diaper on an adult and clean up loose stools and urine. But I did it. Caring for people with disabilities rewards you in ways that can't quite be measured, but you sense that your heart is bigger, and your character deeper.

During that time, I also wrote. I did genealogy research and learned of my family's Jewish roots. I studied Hebrew. I attended and visited churches of various denominations.

I had enjoyed my years as a state trooper. I'd learned much and had proven to myself just what I was capable of doing. However, a mild hearing loss that was first discovered when I was a child had become so profound over the years that, had I tried to stay on the force, I would have gotten someone killed—my partner, a citizen, or me. Things happen for a reason, and, although I was living what appeared to be a bizarre life, it was the right thing to do at the time.

That too, came to an abrupt end, and I once again found myself standing on the street, a small suitcase in my hand and two little dogs I'd acquired huddled securely at my feet. My friend Teri came to get us, and I stayed in her home for two weeks. Other friends had a mobile home in a small town called Alma that they agreed to rent to me. It had a refrigerator and a stove, but was otherwise empty. I slept on the floor with my dogs. The trailer was hot and uncomfortable. Many nights I cried because *this* was something I had difficulty understanding. I felt truly forsaken. I questioned God, screaming and in tears, "Where are you? Show me what I am supposed to do!" There was silence. I was angry that I'd given up my whole life and everything that mattered to me—for nothing, all because I believed I'd heard the voice of God asking me to do so. I didn't mind giving up everything—if there had been a reason. I had expected to be in some manner of ministry by then, but it never happened. That failed expectation was my source of confusion, but I clung to God fiercely in my frustration and fear anyway. I had no car, no job, and I had rent and utilities to pay. I had to start all over. I got part-time jobs doing in-home health care and just enough money trickled in to meet my paltry responsibilities. My big break came when I got a job as a teacher's aide in one of the schools. Finally, I was making big money—seven bucks an hour. Strange, during this whole eight-year phase, I didn't miss horses. They were just gone and no longer a part of my life. I used to lie in bed at 5:30 on winter mornings, thinking of all the crazy horse people out there chopping ice out of buckets. I'd roll over and go back to sleep.

A lot of good things happened that wouldn't have had I not made this drastic life change. I went back to school and earned a bachelor's degree in public administration and then a master's degree in humanities. I wrote to movie director Steven Spielberg and asked to be a part of his world renowned Holocaust project. I was invited to the training in Pennsylvania, quit my job again, and went. The experience was life changing. I came home to interview many Holocaust survivors on film, preserving their stories for the future so that the events might never be forgotten. I interviewed one of the last remaining survivors of the Babi Yar massacre in Kiev, where over thirty thousand Jews were shot and buried in mass graves during two days in September. She had been there. She had seen and she lived to tell about it. One day, she will be gone, but her story will live on.

I fashioned a new life. It was a long, difficult road back to the civilization I had known. Many have privately, and sometimes to my face, ridiculed the choice I made to leave the security I'd known. The fact that it *appeared* to have been for naught didn't help the situation either. I've often looked back and wondered why it all happened. Maybe I was asked to walk away from everything just to see if I would do it. Maybe it wasn't for me to know and never will be. But I came away from that experience with the knowledge that absolutely nothing belongs to me. It *all* belongs to God. We are only passing through and are mere caretakers of the things he chooses to give us. He can take them away at any moment. When all of the dust settles, there are only two things I am sure of: God's intimate involvement in my life, and his complete dominion over all of creation. Need prompts you to pray; faith parts the sea.

I would do it again.

There came some mornings that I would awaken with Zester on my mind. Zester had been my most beloved horse. He was a tall, impressive chestnut with four white socks and a big white blaze. He was my stallion's son. I had given him to a man who promised to keep him forever, so he said. The horse was on my mind too much to ignore it, so I called the man. He'd sold the horse at an auction. I was instantly sick to my stomach at hearing the news. Zester was old by then, and the slaughter market was booming. I spent weeks tracking the horse all over the state from owner to owner. I was so determined to find him and get him back, that I bought a navy blue halter for him and many of the supplies that I would need again for horse ownership. But it wasn't to be the way I had hoped and planned.

Eventually, I found Zester. A woman had just purchased him at yet another auction. I was able to pet him, but she would not sell him to me and chose to sell him to someone else even though I offered her more than twice what she had paid for him. It was, without doubt, the single most heartbreaking experience of my life. I prayed for the horse, but there was nothing more I could do. I learned, much later, that Zester had died.

My small mobile home now had horse stuff accumulating in a corner by the sofa. When I finally accepted that I would never have Zester, I started thinking, *Why not get a horse anyway?*

I found an ad in a paper for a chestnut Arabian mare and called the number listed. The owner's arthritis had become so bad that it was no longer safe for her to continue riding, and she was forced to sell the mare. The woman's name was Connie, and she'd been praying for the right person—hopefully another woman—to take her beloved horse. When I pulled into the driveway of Connie's home, she had the horse in the yard on a lead rope, letting her munch on grass. The petite chestnut mare had four white socks, a big white blaze, and the sweetest disposition. I bought her without ever getting on her back or watching someone else ride her. I found a local place to stable her.

I never intended to ride again. I just knew I needed to have a horse—to brush, to spend time with, to love again. Her name was Maali but I nicknamed her "My Little Angel Girl." One night, in the soft light of the arena, when just the two of us were all alone, I ran my hands over the smoothness of her little back. The next thing I knew, I was standing on a stool, poised and ready to get on her. It had been almost ten years. The moment I sat on her, I was instantly flooded with tears. My body was shaking, and I could not stop crying. Maali just stood there quietly flicking her ears back and looking at me in the calm way horses do. The all-consuming passion for horses rose instantly and filled me. From then on, I rode Maali every day. I bought a western saddle and the rest of the tack I needed.

Maali seemed to miss the companionship of a horse too, so a few months later I found another horse—a black Arabian mare with four white socks named Bonnie. I bought this mare also, and Maali and she became best buddies immediately. I was back into horses full swing, and it was as if I had never been away. I bought another saddle and returned to dressage, the discipline I loved most.

A year later, I opened my mailbox to find an ad for the Great Lakes International Draft Horse Show that takes place every October at the Michigan State University Livestock Pavilion. Strange, I had never heard of this event. Of course, I went.

The moment I saw the draft horses I became that little kid all over again, my head swiveling around so that I didn't miss one horse. Draft horses were everywhere, and, this time, I finally got to touch them.

When I ran my hands over the expanse of a Belgian gelding for the first time, I could barely breathe. I wanted to take all of them home with me.

The draft show horses are huge. Some of them stand well over six feet at the withers, and they are the most powerful living things I've ever seen. Sitting in the bleachers when the six-horse hitches are in the ring, you can feel the seat beneath you rumble as they pass. The "ching, ching" of the tug chains chime rhythmically, like heavy bells. If there are six hitches in the ring, each with six horses that weigh at least twenty-five hundred pounds a piece, that totals ninety thousand pounds—*forty-five tons* of horseflesh in the ring at the same time.

I love my Arabians. I have some appaloosas and a palomino now, and I love them all. In fact, there has yet to be a horse created that I don't love, but it's different with Belgians. They own my heart.

In time, another childhood dream came true. I did get to have my Belgian draft horse, and it was wonderful.

This is his story.

CHAPTER
Three

I'D HEARD ABOUT THE old Belgian gelding, but I never went to see him until one sunny afternoon in October. My friend Susan, who owned the barn where my horses were stabled, and her seven-year-old daughter Kelly and I drove out to see him. We found him standing alone in a field. One low strand of flopping wire partially encircled an otherwise vacant pasture. The lone wire certainly wasn't sufficient to keep a pony contained, let alone a horse his size, if he'd wanted to escape. I parked on the side of the road, slid out of my truck, and parted the overgrown ragweed and burdock in the ditch in order to get close to the fence. Either the horse didn't notice me, or he just didn't care that I was there. So, I started to pace back and forth, waving my arms, calling, "Hey horse" and flashing fists full of grass to coax him over to me. In between flailing my arms and picking more enticing wads of grass, I noticed a weathered, white mobile home in the pasture that was covered with elephant-sized dents. It sat crooked, obviously towed there and left to rot away.

I was just about to give up on getting the horse to come to me, when his head began to lift slowly and mechanically, like a child's toy low on battery juice, barely acknowledging my intrusive theatrics. Inch by slow inch, he turned his whole body around and began shuffling toward me. His head hung close to his knees, and his body plodded along like an ancient, moss-covered turtle crossing a road. He barely picked each hoof up long enough to propel himself forward before it was pulled back to earth. Though he walked toward me, his body was slightly angled to the left. Not wanting him to shy, I stood motionless, offering words of encouragement: "You can do it; come on, boy, come and get some of this nice grass."

It took so long for him to lumber up to the fence that it could have snowed before he reached me. I figured that the old horse had come over to me not because he was interested, but out of obedience. He stood quietly next to the wobbly old fence. His head remained down, each large, bug-bitten ear limply cast to the side. Burs had long ago conquered his mane and fashioned it into one grotesque solid clump. His forelock was so stiff with sticks and cockleburs that it stuck straight out, like a unicorn's horn. His eyes were swollen and nearly shut; only two slits on either side of his head hinted that vision hadn't deserted him entirely. He was drooling profusely. The horse perked up just enough to reach across the wire and touch my outstretched hand with his flaccid muzzle. Instantaneously, a bolt of warmth shot up my arm and deposited itself neatly and firmly into my heart. I knew at that moment that the horse would somehow spend the rest of his days with me.

I knocked on several doors of nearby homes before I found someone who knew the owner of the horse. At the third home, a lady told me the farmer who owned him was out in a field on his tractor. "See that tractor way out in the field?" She pointed. "That's Joe; he owns the horse." I thanked her and went to the edge of the field, waiting until almost dark before the tractor grumbled its way over to me and I was finally able to speak to Joe.

"I was told you own that Belgian gelding. Is that right?" I asked.

"Yes I do. Why do you want to know?"

"Would you ever consider selling him?"

The well-sun-ripened farmer sighed, took off his cap, scratched among scattered gray hairs on his head, and said, "I've been thinking of taking him to an auction."

Horrified, I blurted out, "Do you realize he would go straight to slaughter?"

"Yeah," Joe said. "But then I'd know for sure what happened to him. I don't want someone getting him and trying to make him pull or work hard. He's too old for ..."

"Would you sell him to me?" I interrupted.

The farmer sat quietly atop his puttering red tractor for a few moments, then shut the ignition off and jumped down. "He'd probably bring five hundred bucks at an auction," he said. "I'll sell him to you for five hundred."

Under the opaque moonlight of a dusky October sky, we shook hands on the deal. The horse would have to stay on Joe's property until I could get my veterinarian to draw blood for the Coggins Test that all horses are required to have before they can leave their farms. Joe told me the horse's name was Don. And now Don was my horse.

It would take about a week for the results of the test to come back. I could barely get to sleep each night, thinking that my horse, Don, was waiting to come home. Until then, I went out to visit with the horse every day to get to know him.

On my first trip to Don's home, from a distance, I saw the mobile home rocking back and forth as if it were a toy. When I pulled up beside the pasture, Don was scratching his colossal shoulders on the side of trailer, heaving the structure with each shove. I shook my head and smiled; this creative old horse had invented a convenient use for some human's junk. The dents hadn't been created by elephants, but they were mighty impressive indeed.

I usually found Don standing in his pasture with his head down, drooling and oblivious to all that went on around him. I sensed that he was merely living out his days and that he'd given up on life. An infrequent swish of his tail was about all that indicated that there might be a pulse coursing through his body. There was nothing for him to do and no reason for him to make an attempt to find something of interest. He'd shut everything out.

I first attempted to bribe Don by offering him large Red Delicious apples that I handpicked from the fresh produce section at the grocery store. At first, he only sniffed them and turned his head away. Just as humans aren't born with a taste for coffee, horses have to learn to appreciate apples. I assumed he had never had an apple, so I bit into one and poked a piece of it between his wrinkled pink lips. He nodded his head up and down as horses do when they eat something they aren't familiar with. But then, his eyes opened a little more, and I could almost feel the old, beloved memories as they tumbled back into the horse. Don had long forgotten the sweet joy of an apple.

By my next visit, Don wasn't in his usual spot in the middle of the pasture. He was standing a few feet away from the fence. I got out of my truck and called, "Hey boy." He cast his ears forward lazily, as one might toss a pebble in the direction of a stream. He made a low, deep rumble that I came to translate as, "Hello there, little lady."

The old fellow moseyed over to me with his slow sideways steps. He thrust his hooves forward and down, heavy and deliberate. I burst into peels of belly-deep laughter; Don looked and sounded like an equine version of John Wayne.

On the third day, I could see that Don was waiting by the fence. There was another car in front of me, and I watched as Don's head went up and his ears shot forward, hoping. The car passed by without stopping, and Don's head immediately sunk back down to his knees as if lamenting, "She won't come anymore." But I did appear, and, when he heard my voice, Don realized that I was coming to see him—and I would always come back. He greeted me with his soft, low rumble, and, from that point on, I was his girl. This was a breakthrough. I put my arms around Don's big, cresty neck as he stood motionless, yet free to leave. He chose to stay.

I spent hours combing Don's mane, tail, and forelock until all the burs were gone and had drifted away on a breeze to wherever it is that burs are supposed to go. Don had a glorious golden-white mane. It hung to his shoulders and was so thick that it draped over both sides of his neck. His forelock was equally profuse and spilled down his face, almost to the end of his muzzle. Most Belgians have docked tails, but Don's was intact, and so long that it brushed the ground. After he had endured several days of brushing, the sun began to make attempts to dance on his copper-colored coat where there were scattered, subtle hints of shine emerging in the wake of the currycomb.

The veterinarian had said Don's eyes were closed and swollen from burdock seeds, but they were otherwise healthy. I brought out a thermos of warm water and rinsed his eyes. Once they were open and clear, I could see that they were full of life and sparkling with kindness and intelligence.

We always had apples during our visits. Those of us who have Arabians know that, with their delicate little muzzles, the fruit must be cut into quarters. This was not required with Don. An entire apple offered to him on my hand would vanish. Once, he insisted on stuffing two apples into his mouth at the same time. His cheeks bulged and applesauce slobbered until it gushed onto the ground, but he managed to juice the apples sufficiently to swallow the mush. When there were no more apples and it was time for me to leave for the day, Don would nuzzle my pockets and my hands, searching for one last treat.

Farmer Joe told me that Don had belonged to his wife's uncle. The horse had been important in his prime and "meant the world" to the man who had owned him. Don had spent his early years yanking stumps out of the woods and working as a logger. He had also pulled wagons in parades when he wasn't formally on duty. Joe said that Don loved his job and seemed to pride himself in being the strongest horse in the area. Neighboring farmers often got together and had backyard horse-pulling contests. No horse was a match for Don; he easily beat them all. When the uncle passed away, Joe inherited Don, but had no real use for him, so he just left him in the pasture to stand alone with nothing to do. The horse was now seventeen years old, and he had been idle and without the company of another horse for twelve years.

Don's blood test cleared him to travel. Though it still seemed like a dream, it began to settle into my heart that Don truly was my horse, and I wanted him with me as quickly as possible.

I arranged for a commercial livestock hauler to meet me at Don's home. The horse was fitted with an old, faded red nylon halter, stiff from age and held together with a huge rusty pin. Don paused when asked to step through the wire gate leaving his pasture. He hadn't been out of that enclosure for twelve years, and, being a well-behaved horse, he wasn't sure if he should violate the rules. I held a wad of grass in my hand in front of him as a bribe, and Don stepped through the gate, and into his new life. The rig was parked in the road, and the old horse hopped up into the trailer without quibble and quietly rode the short distance to the barn. I followed, each rotation of my truck tires steadily increasing my exuberance. I imagined all of the great and wonderful things I would be able to do with my Belgian. I planned to take him on trail rides and maybe even take him on the ride that crossed the state. I envisioned my new horse pulling a beautiful carriage, complete with fringe on top.

When we reached the barn where my horses lived and I asked Don to step down from the trailer, he hesitated. Although he could see the ground, his ears twitched nervously back and forth, and he eyed both the ground and me, trying to assess the safety of the situation. Don was aware of his age, and, like an elderly person, he was afraid of falling. I asked him to come out of the trailer again. This time, he carefully set a front foot onto the ground, testing its security, and then the rest of him followed. He promptly proceeded to drag me all around the yard, whinnying as if to proclaim, "Horses! There are horses here!"

He could smell them. He could hear their whinnies. He flung his head and pranced and danced, tugging me along with every sprawling step he took. I tried to brace my legs in resistance, but they were as useless as toothpicks against the force of a hurricane. I was tossed along, taking scrambling steps to try to keep up with him—or else end up being dragged like a shoestring on a very big boot.

"Whoa, whoa!" I hollered, but it was like trying to navigate a crippled 747 as it careens recklessly over the ground. After crashing over and smashing several shrubs and disrupting rocks, Don towed me up to the barn. Here, he came to an abrupt, frozen halt and stared at the building.

Don had never been in a barn in his life, and he wasn't convinced that now was the time to start. Heavy-duty coaxing with apples and grain held just close enough to him so that he could smell them, but just far enough away that his lips smacked futilely, finally prompted him to set his feet inside. Once in the barn, he heard whinnies and immediately concluded that it was a safe place.

Don desperately wanted to meet the other horses, but the first meeting with my mares was not particularly pleasant. I turned Don loose in the small arena with Maali and Bonnie. The old gelding walked friskily toward Maali, anxious to meet her. Maali merely turned her body away and ignored him as if he were nothing more than a fly on a fence post. Bonnie, however, approached him with her elegant neck arched and her petite ears forward. They touched outstretched noses briefly and then Bonnie immediately squealed, spun around and planted one of her dainty little white hooves smack-dab in the middle of his muzzle. I heard the thud. Don stood there for a few moments, wiggling his stinging lips surely thinking, "That little one sure packs a wallop."

That first day, Susan and I decided to put Don in cross ties, which are ropes or chains that run from each side of a barn isle to the center where the horse is hooked, one rope on each side of the halter. These were heavy-duty chains. The intent was to look him over and brush him, but we learned quite abruptly that Don had never been in cross ties in his life, and he didn't understand that he was supposed to stand still while we worked with him. Don started moving those heavy feet. His big body pressed forward, and the chains were pulled so taught that there was no way to release them. Quickly, Susan and I both propped our shoulders against his heavy chest, bracing against his strength.

"How do you make him stop?" Susan asked in a panic-stricken voice, the wood of her barn creaking as the chains pulled tighter from the walls. Our bodies popped forward with each step Don took as if we were mere Tinker Toys.

"I don't know ... I don't know!" I wailed. "Whoa, whoa!"

Then we did what anyone would do in the same situation. We got the giggles. "Just like Lucy and Ethel," I rasped. We were seized by laughter to the point of utter incapacitation.

Seconds before the chains would have ripped from the barn walls, the great hulk of a horse came to a stop. Susan and I were instantly silenced, and I stealthily grabbed Don's halter and asked him to back up. He obediently marched a few steps back so that the chains hung slack on each side. Then we unhooked the chains and tied him up instead.

The first day at the barn came to an end, and I went home ecstatic that I finally owned a Belgian—a very old one that probably wouldn't live much more than a year. Still, he *was* a Belgian, my first draft horse. I jabbered on the phone for most of the night, sharing the news with friends. I couldn't sleep. I grinned and laughed out loud and danced around the house chanting, "I own a Belgian; I own a Belgian." I prayed and dedicated the horse to the Lord and thanked him for letting me have Don. I told him that Don was his horse and that I would be content just being his caretaker.

That first night as a draft horse owner, I was reminded of the Ronnie Milsap song, "I Wouldn't Have Missed It for the World." Even though the lyrics are about a girl, the title seemed to fit my relationship with Don. I thought about all of the people who had driven by the lonely horse over the years. Apparently, no one had stopped to ask about him but me. They had missed their chance. I was the one who had him now, and getting to know him more each day was something I knew I'd never regret.

In the mix of giddiness and exhaustion that night, I had a dream. It was a dream that anchored my belief that Don was meant to be my horse. In the dream, there were two old horsemen sitting side by side in heaven drinking coffee. One was Don's original owner.

"I got a Belgian horse down there that my family is thinking about sending to an auction," he said, taking a sip from his steaming cup.

"And I've got a kid down there who has always wanted a Belgian," my father said. "Why don't we get them together?"

And so it was.

CHAPTER
Four

MANY YEARS AGO, BEFORE my parents were married, my mother wanted to learn the name of a man she saw walking a German shepherd dog by her house. The handsome young man would pass by, chewing on a timothy stalk, with the dog faithfully by his side.

"That's Rin," people told her.

His *nickname* was "Rin," for Rin Tin Tin, the famous canine hero, but the correct pronunciation was lost in the Upper Peninsula accent, and my mother thought they were saying "Ren." The name Ren stuck for the rest of my father's life; no one in my family ever called him by his real name, which was Eric. I have always loved the name Ren, and it seemed only fitting to change Don's name to Ren. I knew my father had somehow managed to guide me to this horse and he would have been overjoyed to have such a grand horse named after him.

Ren had never been abused, but he hadn't had much attention for many years, and I was sure his teeth were in poor condition. I surmised that his teeth had never been examined, let alone floated (smoothed with a file). So, I called Doug, my horse dentist, to come out and check Ren's choppers.

My new horse impressed me with his pleasant attitude. He greeted everyone he met with uncanny hospitality, like a sweet grandfather who automatically and unquestioningly is the first person to extend his right hand for a shake. Ren was genuine. He liked everyone and everything. Nothing seemed to faze him or worry him. I could do anything with him, and he just didn't care. It was no different for Doug when he came to work on Ren's teeth.

"Bring him out in the isle and put him in the cross ties," Doug said.

I brought my horse out of his stall, glanced at those flimsy logging chains for a few seconds, and remembered our previous experience with them. Slowly and carefully, I hooked each chain to Ren's halter, thinking that, if he didn't notice they were attached, perhaps he wouldn't attempt to walk away, pulling chunks of the barn walls with him. But Ren kept his body motionless, only shaking his head up and down to make the chains rattle. On his own, he had decided that, when he was hooked to these odd, floppy things, he was supposed to stand quietly. He never pulled on them again.

Doug placed the speculum, the piece of equipment used to crank open a horse's jaws, over Ren's head and into his mouth. Once it was in place, Doug was able to put his hands into the horse's mouth up to his elbows and conduct a thorough examination without worrying about jaws that could grind rocks into powder clamping down onto his arms.

"What did you find?" I asked, nervously.

"He definitely needs work. Got some bad hooks on the teeth he has left," Doug said.

"What do you do about those?"

"I cut 'em off," he said.

Doug released the speculum and allowed the horse to relax before he began the actual work. As Doug stroked the horse's face, Ren began sniffing him up and down his legs, his shoulders, and his neck, and he nuzzled his hands. Ren seemed entranced. I had no idea at the time that the horse was disclosing an important part of his personality.

Doug filled a bucket with water, assembled his tools near him, and placed the dental halter and speculum back on Ren's head. He inserted large rasps, called floats, into the horse's mouth. Doug braced his body, keeping his eyes focused on the horse's eyes, and began filing. Ren leaned his body into Doug and tilted his head at slightly different angles throughout the process.

"They seem to know that I'm helping them," Doug said. "They try to help me find the bad spots."

Doug slid a large, two-handed pair of nippers into Ren's mouth, and there was an awful cracking sound as he cut each hook. He handed me one of the dark yellow chunks of tooth; it was almost as long as a section of my finger.

"What would that be like for a horse to have those?" I asked.

"He's most likely had a bad headache—a really *bad* headache—for a good decade or so," Doug said.

Tears immediately welled in my eyes as I thought about the pain my sweet horse must have been in. When I have a headache, I expect the whole world to stop and find me something to make it go away. Ren's only option had been to suffer in silence.

"How old did you say this horse is?" Doug quickly and wisely asked, just before my tears spilled over.

"I was told about seventeen," I said, blinking my eyes and clearing my throat.

"Let's say middle twenties," Doug said, grinning broadly.

"No way!" I exclaimed. "Draft horses don't live that long."

"This one did," Doug said. "I'd call him twenty-five. He's probably one of the oldest draft horses in Michigan. He's certainly the oldest one I've worked on."

While Doug continued to work on Ren, I grew quiet as I contemplated what I'd gotten myself into. I had wanted a Belgian so badly, but the one I ended up with was much older than I had been told. Since he had already exceeded the expected life span of a draft horse, it was disheartening to think I could lose him at almost any hour. I had prayed for a Belgian, and I could almost hear the Lord saying, "You didn't say you wanted a *young* one."

Another loud snap of the nippers jolted me back into the moment as the last hook was severed. Ren was rolling his tongue outside of his mouth and smacking his lips, obviously feeling the difference, and feeling very good.

"How many teeth are in there?" I asked.

"Not too many," Doug said. "He has all of his front teeth, but he's lost some of his molars."

"Can he still eat okay?"

"Yeah, he's in good flesh," Doug said. "He can't be having too many problems. I'd let him use what he's got and let him eat what he can for now."

Doug finished up with Ren, smoothing out the last rough areas with the floats. It had taken two hours to complete the work, and Ren had been patient, interested, and a perfect gentleman the entire time. When Doug had rinsed his tools and was packed up ready to go to his next appointment, Ren rubbed his face and forehead against Doug's shoulder, all the while smacking his lips in the most sincere display of gratitude.

"To think, some people say horses are dumb," Doug said, chuckling and patting Ren loudly on his neck. If Ren had been able, he would have hugged Doug, and picked him up and bounced him all around the barnyard the way football players do when they're rejoicing over a touchdown.

Ren was immediately changed after his dental appointment. When I turned him loose in his pasture, he broke into a playful trot, tossing his head and strutting along the fence line, feeling like a fresh, young colt again. He was free from years of pain that I couldn't begin to imagine. He never drooled again.

That night, I explained to the Lord that Ren was considerably older than I had thought. I asked to have more time with him. Since he was an aged horse, being allowed to have him for ten years wasn't likely. Two seemed more reasonable, so that's what I asked for.

Ren began his life with me by easing into the distinction of being a "special-needs" horse. Quite often, when he ate hay, he choked on it. The stiff, poorly chewed stems would puncture his esophagus and he would bleed from the nostrils. He spent the first year with a nasal discharge, which I learned is common in horses who choke. I hand selected softer sections of hay so that it would go down easier. I mixed up a special feed for him that consisted of soft, crimped oats, a little sweet feed, and vitamins. It was like a horse version of trail mix. The special concoction worked for a few months, and then I noticed that the oats were passing right through him. He just didn't have enough teeth to properly grind up the grains that younger horses eat. I had to find something else for him. I found just what Ren needed the next time I went to the mill where I buy most of my horse feed and supplies.

"Do you have a feed specially made for old horses?" I asked Joel, the manager.

"Sure, there are quite a few brands," he said, pulling out some pamphlets from a drawer.

"Some people really like Purina's Equine Senior."

We read the list of ingredients together, and Joel pointed out that it was a complete feed, meaning it contained everything that an older horse required nutritionally in the shape of neat little pellets. It even had hay processed and compressed into those pellets. It smelled wonderfully sweet, and the morsels were soft enough to squish with my fingers and slightly sticky to make it easier for the dentally challenged to chew.

"All a horse really has to do is get it in his mouth, and it pretty well breaks down. It's almost like it's predigested," Joel said. "We sell a lot of it."

With his advice, I bought a fifty-pound bag and took it home to Ren.

When I arrived at the barn, Ren tossed his head at the sound of my voice, his mane cresting sharply like a wave reaching up for the sun. He nickered and jogged over to me. Ren was never in a hurry about anything unless he assumed food was involved. All horses love to eat, but Ren *really* loved his food.

After I'd dumped a serving into the black, sawed-in-half, fifty-gallon drum that served as his feed tub, Ren only needed about two seconds to determine if the stuff was edible. He dove right in and did not raise his head until the Equine Senior was gone. Then he licked the tub until it was well polished and shiny, and expected more. This was the perfect feed for my old horse. It had everything he needed and Ren would no longer get hay. It was heart wrenching, though, for me to watch him when my mares got their flakes of hay. He waited at the fence, ears twitching in worry, but no hay came. There was no way to help him understand why he was no longer getting his precious stems. All he knew was that he wanted it, just like the other horses. He'd eaten hay all of his life, and now, suddenly, it was gone. His big heart was breaking. It was too sad for me to watch. I knew I had to find some way to feed him hay.

I made phone calls to friends, local horse people, and feed stores, asking if anyone knew of a soft type of hay for sale. Someone gave me the name of a farmer who lived about forty miles away who had soft-textured, second-cutting, grass hay. The next day, I drove to his farm and examined it. As soon as I saw it, I knew it would be perfect; it was a deep green color, smelled clean and fresh, and was so soft that I thought about slathering it in bleu cheese salad dressing and eating it myself.

I returned home with two of the bales to see how Ren would do with it before I bought a larger supply. When I approached Ren with a few flakes perched on my arm, he came at it open-jawed, teeth positioned for the kill, and latched onto it, cramming as much into his mouth as he could possibly hold. He had so much hay in his mouth that he could barely make his jaws move.

With his mouth jammed, Ren glared at me while he chewed; only taking his eyes off me when he dipped his head down to vacuum up the next wad. I laughed with tears in my eyes; it was both comical and sad to see him so happy over something as simple as hay. From then on, I made the trip once a month to get the special forage that Ren was able to chew or gum sufficiently enough to swallow safely.

Almost on a daily basis, Ren did something that either made me laugh, or cry. I never knew what I'd find when I went to the barn. One day, as my truck approached, I noticed the overhead power cables and boxes swaying. I pulled into the driveway to find Ren scratching those heavy shoulders on the telephone pole in his pasture with enough power to rattle the cables. I called the power company when I got back home.

"Is it okay if my horse is scratching his neck and shoulders on a telephone pole?"

"Sure, deer do it all the time," the man on the other end said.

"I need to tell you that this horse weighs about two thousand pounds, and, when he does this, all of the lines and those gray boxes overhead wobble."

There was a long pause.

"That probably isn't a good idea," the man said.

After that, the telephone pole was sectioned off with a strand of wire fencing so that Ren couldn't reach it. When he returned to this favorite scratching spot, he inspected the intrusive addition, walked away, and found something else to do. Ren was never one to get bogged down by change, and he shunned disappointment.

My elderly companion enjoyed being brushed and fussed over, and it wasn't long before he began to blossom; his mane and tail were clean and silky, his red-chestnut body hair gleamed in the sunlight, and his muzzle was no longer wrinkled. He always sauntered slightly sideways like that famous cowboy, but there was more bounce and impulsion to his gait. He'd developed a salty swagger that seemed to imply that he could do more. I didn't know if Ren had ever been ridden, but he had made so much progress that, one day, I decided to try it. It had always been my dream to ride my own Belgian draft horse.

It's safer and wiser to start any new horse with an unknown past by introducing the saddle and doing all of the necessary groundwork before the first ride. But Ren's laid-back attitude about everything encouraged me to bypass all of that. I knew that it would never occur to Ren to buck or bolt.

I heaved my Arabian western saddle up onto his back, tightened up the cinch, and abruptly stopped as I stared at how the stirrups sprung up and out to the sides like the Flying Nun's wing-like coronet. There was no way I'd be able to get my foot into the stirrup because it was about level with my eyes. How was I going to get up there? I had to think creatively. I got a stepstool and then a garbage can that I overturned. I placed them side by side near Ren. All this time, the horse stood patiently, waiting for me to figure out my plans. I climbed up to the top step on the stool and then stepped onto the garbage can and hoisted myself onto the saddle. The first time I sat up on his massive back, I felt that old, near-breathless excitement flood into me right down to my toes. This was my first time on the back of a draft horse. I was atop a mystical mountain, looking down at the rest of the world beneath me. Ren only looked back at me once to see if I'd disappeared. His eyes blinked and appeared to get larger when he located me in such a strange place. Most likely, it was the first time he'd had a person on his back. Ren nuzzled my pant leg, satisfied that everything was okay. When I squeezed his sides, he moved off at a walk as if he'd been doing it all his life. As he strode forward, his blond crest flexed, heavily listing from side to side as he used his neck. I was commandeering the original version of the army tank—a living remnant of the most elite, ancient war transport. That first ride was short; after only a few laps around the arena, I decided that was enough for our first time. I was proud of Ren for accepting something so new and strange without any fuss.

Getting off Ren's back also posed a unique challenge, and, for a while, I was stuck up there as I contemplated the situation. Trying to position him near my obstacle course of mounting aids was too tedious, and trying to lower myself by balancing on the shaky garbage can didn't seem safe. I knew if I tried to just jump down, I'd fracture most of the old bones in my body from the jolt. Instead, I swung my right leg over the horse, held onto the saddle horn and cantle, and carefully oozed down to the ground, like a garden slug descending over the edge of a sun-warmed rock. It worked, and that's how I got off him every time I dismounted from then on.

Ren had arthritis in his knees, and, though he never limped, he did stumble occasionally. When we went for a ride, I had to be content to walk and maybe jog only a few steps on safe, flat terrain. It just isn't safe to ride a horse who stumbles on its front end beyond much more than a walk. After a few practice rides in the small arena over the next two weeks, I had learned what would cause Ren to stumble. If I asked him to turn slowly and didn't ask him to trot too fast, I could avoid most missteps. But soon, riding in circles in the arena at only a walk became boring for both me and the horse. I decided it was time to take Ren for a ride outside.

Our first trail ride was richly enveloped in a typical Michigan fall afternoon; golden and red leaves flashed against the lucid blue sky, and the scent of warm earth rose to greet us.

It started out as a perfect ride. Ren walked with purpose; his head was up and his ears were forward. He was enjoying the adventure as much as I was. The pungent aroma of a slightly sweaty horse fused with the sweet smell of leather and drifted lazily up to me. I closed my eyes to feel the warm sunshine on my face, breathe, and take in the rich mixture of senses as we walked along a path.

The neighbors raised miniature horses, and their pasture was filled with a herd of at least ten of the little creatures. I was quite confident that Ren had probably seen almost everything because cars didn't bother him, and dogs didn't bother him either. However, when the entire herd of miniature horses turned and headed in our direction, I felt Ren's body tense. The minis zoomed toward us as fast as their bitty legs could carry them, whinnying all the way. They trotted in our direction, eager to meet another horse, but Ren must not have recognized them as his own species. All he was able to quickly determine was that it was a dangerous pack of knee-high potential predators coming to get him. The muscles in his back and neck became rigid when the minis got within about thirty feet of us. Ren whirled and started to trot a few steps away, most likely planning to turn around to have another look, as horses do. But in the confusion, and in trying to move too quickly, he stumbled and could not recover. His neck lurched forward, and we crashed down in a matter of seconds like an imploded skyscraper. I was catapulted out of the saddle while Ren did a complete somersault, missing me with his full body weight by mere inches as he thundered to the earth with a sickening groan. He scrambled to his feet, jogged several strides away, then stopped and stood, twitching his ears and snorting. He was bewildered. It was probably the first time that Ren had ever fallen. It was the worst fall I'd ever had from a horse. I remained flat on back and motionless for several minutes before I tried to rise. My head hurt, and, as I felt it, I found leaves and sticks tangled in my hair. The red bandana I'd had around my head was gone, never to be found. As I lay on the ground, pain seeped into my left hip, my back, and my neck. My shoulder throbbed as if someone were wailing on it with a sledgehammer. I slowly got up from the dirt and staggered over to Ren. I collected the loose reins, petted Ren, spoke softly to him, and checked him for injuries. He was not injured, but I had re-injured a torn rotator cuff, and I was nauseated from the pain. Away from my stepstool and garbage can, there was no way to get back on my horse, so we walked together back to the barn, with me leaning against him for support. During the walk, I had time to realize that I could have been killed from the dramatic toss out of the saddle, or from the ton of horseflesh that had just missed landing on top of my body. I knew that I would have to be content to have Ren as a big pet. It was not safe to ride him. Though I still got on him bareback now and then and sat up there, enjoying the view from on top of the world, I abandoned the urge to take him trail riding. He wasn't steady enough on his front legs to take the chance of another fall.

Ren always wanted to be involved in everything that was going on. He wanted to be with the other horses as a true member of a herd. But my two Arabian mares resented him; he was an outsider, and they treated him as such. On the first day, when the three of them were out in pasture, Maali would make him stand in the corner all by himself while Bonnie ate hay. Maali would face him, flatten her ears tightly against her head, and curl her lips. She looked like a little witch, and Ren wasn't about to cross her. Then Bonnie would come and relieve Maali, and Maali would get to go to one of the hay piles. They took turns making him stand in the corner. Having spent so many years alone and without the company of another horse, Ren wanted to belong so earnestly that he was willing to put up with their acidic dispositions to just be near them. Eventually, the fun and newness of being mean wore off. Both mares ignored him, and he was free to walk around in the pasture. It almost seemed impossible that a horse so large could be intimidated by two little mares who didn't weigh as much together as he did on his own, but it never occurred to Ren to challenge their authority. There was no room in Ren's mind for aggression, and there was no need in his heart for conflict. He accepted everything that life tossed his way.

It was frustrating for me to own horses and have them stabled on someone else's property. Having owned and cared for horses all of my life, I wanted things done my way. I was fortunate and always managed to find stall space or barns to rent so that I could do all of the work myself. I wanted to be the one to feed my horses, and I insisted on supplying my own grain and hay. I would come out at least twice a day to do chores, and I spent hours at a time working with my horses. Most stable owners weren't prepared for that level of dedication. It was a constant heartache for me to leave them at the end of the day, like saying goodnight to your children and then tucking them into someone else's bed in someone else's home. In the span of five years, my horses were at eight different barns. I'd usually stay for a few months at one barn and then become frustrated, pack up, and move somewhere else. Many nights I cried, begging the Lord for a place of our own. I wanted to see my horses right outside my window. More than anything else, when the time came, I wanted to be able to bury Ren on my own property.

For much of my life, I was in pursuit of grand things. I wanted to change the world, fix its problems, and make it a better place. Some people get to do that. Most of us don't. I was able to do a lot, though; I had been a state trooper, interviewed Holocaust survivors on film, and worked as an advocate for victims of domestic violence. I had taught in colleges and was a published free-lance writer. Still, I was always chasing something bigger and better. I applied for numerous lofty jobs, including those at the United Nations and some in Washington DC. All of those delusions of grandeur peeled away on one rainy day with Ren. I was long-lining him—walking behind him, as if driving him—in the indoor arena. I wondered how I would be able to do all of those grand things with Ren in my life. When you walk behind a draft horse, you cannot see anything directly in front of you, beyond the horse's haunches, so I watched as his hip muscles flexed and tensed, shifting powerfully with each step. There was nothing else to do but watch, and think. In that solitude of shuffling around the dirt arena, I thought about my future and asked myself some questions.

"Would Ren be able to make a long-distance trip?"

"Is it fair to do that to this old horse?"

"What if I have to travel a lot? Who will care for Ren? Who could I trust?"

I thought about where I'd been during the course of my life and the things that mattered most to my heart. When is it ever enough? When is it okay to stop, look around, and decide that *this is good*? When is it okay to accept your life and not feel pressured to chase after more than you need? I had arthritis and a spine that was disintegrating. I was going deaf, had a host of other medical concerns, and was approaching fifty years of age—and still, I felt that it was my responsibility to solve all of the world's problems. My mind continually pressured me that I needed to do everything. Yet there I was, walking along behind Ren in the quiet and peace of a horse's world. My life had been entrenched in horses, and the simplicity of their world and the simplicity of *this* horse's world filled me with real and satisfying joy.

A smile began to crease my worried face. It was the kind of smile that begins somewhere deep in your soul and ripens slowly, like a sly June rose, until it's in full bloom.

"Maybe this is enough," I said out loud. "Maybe walking behind this big old horse butt is enough." At that moment, I was able to let go of the grandiose goals that had never been placed within my reach in the first place.

I knew that Ren was supposed to be my horse. I knew I was supposed to fetch him out of that pasture and give him a life again. It didn't start out that way, but, day by day, Ren became a special horse to me. It wasn't until the time came to turn around and look back that the fullness and worth of this experience became clear.

He needed me.

CHAPTER
Five

AFTER ALMOST TWO YEARS at that barn, we moved to barn number two. A man named Paul and his wife Ellen owned the new place. They had sold their horses years ago and bought a cabin instead. They had no use for the barn now, so they agreed to rent it to me. It was all set up for draft horses, with huge, fourteen-by-fourteen-foot stalls and several paddocks. I had the barn all to myself, and it was a good place.

Although I no longer rode Ren, I felt he still needed a job. Horses, just like people, need jobs. They are happier and thrive when they feel needed and have purpose. Once we had settled into the new barn, I decided that we would go for walks down the road. It would be good for both of us and give us something that we could do together. Every day, weather permitting, Ren and I walked about a mile down the road, turned around and came back. He was not fond of leaving the barn and would whinny and try to walk sideways down the driveway in hopes that I'd give in and let him stay home. Even though the mares didn't like him, they were still his herd, and he wanted to stay with them. Once we made it to the road, Ren settled down and calmly walked beside me. Our walks were always at a near snail pace, relaxing, and required no mental effort.

One day, after we'd walked about a mile from the barn, Ren planted his frying-pan-sized hooves in the middle of the road and stopped. It was the narrowest part of the road, and he refused to move. He didn't want to walk any farther, and he didn't want to walk home either. He had made an executive decision to stand crossways in the middle of the road and go to sleep. Nothing I did budged him. I pushed on him with my shoulders to coax him into taking a step—*any* step, in *any* direction—just to get us moving again. I reefed on his lead rope to the left and to the right, trying to throw him off balance in the hope of forcing him to move. I leaned my full body weight back against the lead rope until it was pulled taught between us. I even swatted him on the butt with the loose end of the rope.

"Come on, Ren, let's go!" I said.

Ren's only response was to calmly close his eyes and let his lower lip dangle loosely. His ears slowly drifted apart and down to the sides of his head, like nearly deflated birthday balloons.

"Hey lady, can you move your horse so I can get by?"

I nearly jumped out of my boots. A man was sitting in a white Ford pickup just on the other side of us. A hot, tomato blush emblazoned my face instantly. I didn't know how long the man had been watching, but the subtle, sideways grin on his face let me know that he was more amused than angry. Gosh, I was embarrassed; I was a skilled horsewoman, and these kinds of things never happened to me. I glanced at my horse. Ren had become very comfortable and was resting a hind foot, dozing in the warm summer sunshine.

"I'm trying to move him, but he won't budge." I sighed.

Leaning back against the seat in his truck, as if settling into a favorite easy chair to watch an old movie, the man lit a cigarette.

"Why won't he move?" he asked, after taking a puff.

"I don't know. I've never had this problem with him before," I stammered. I tugged on the lead rope once again and gave him a slap on the rump as proof of my effort—and dilemma. Ren smacked his lips and cracked his eyes open just enough to hint that he'd been disturbed, and then closed his eyes again.

I glanced around Ren's body. There was just enough room for the driver to ease his truck on past the horse if he went slowly and carefully.

"I think you can make it." I motioned with my chin. "Over there."

"Lady, you want me to drive behind the business end of that horse?" he asked.

"He's never kicked, ever," I said.

"Yeah, but you said you've never had the problem of him stalling either."

"I don't know what else to tell you. We'll be here till he decides to move," I said. I could feel flames of red spreading from my chest clear to my ears.

The half smile twitched on the man's face again. He sat up, flicked his cigarette butt out the window, and began to inch his truck forward, partially off the road and into the ditch, never taking his eyes of that ample, red rump until he made it to the other side.

"Good luck," the man called out as the Ford cleared the horse and began to pick up speed. I watched as the truck grew tinier and tinier, coaxing waves of dust with it, until it had disappeared.

When the sandy film had settled and the road returned to deserted quiet, we were still standing in the same spot in the middle of the road. I couldn't get the horse to move, and I couldn't leave him. There was nothing to do but wait it out. It wasn't for another ten minutes that my luck changed. Suddenly, Ren awoke and decided that he would like to go home, so home we went. Puffs of weightless dust rose in the dry summer dirt with each step as his heavy hooves churned us with steadily increasing speed toward the barn. I was jogging to keep up with him. I kept glancing up at Ren, wondering what had gotten into him. I'd never seen him behave so strangely, first stopping in the road and now doing a good imitation of a trotter on the track. He announced that he had returned to the barn with a loud, triumphant whinny to impress the Girls. I was out of breath and panting. Holding a horse—or being nearly dragged by a horse—through deep road dust and trying to keep up with him was a lot of work. Exhausted and trying to catch my breath, I plastered my body to the side of the barn for support and let go of the lead rope. Ren trotted into the barn. I heard crashing noises as he tipped over a trash can and stepped on it. I heard the sound of pails singing through the air as Ren bulled his way around the barn, searching for the treats he knew were hiding somewhere just out of his reach. He was moving quickly, knowing that at any moment I would come and put an end to his expedition. It was his one chance, and, by golly, he was going to make the most of it. I chuckled and shook my head, perplexed at the crazy antics I'd just been a part of.

Life with Ren was certainly a hoot.

At this barn, there was an indoor wash rack for horses. It was doubtful that Ren had ever had a bath in his life, but on one hot July day, I decided to give him his first good scrubbing. I tied Ren up on the cement wash rack and got my stepstool, hose, shampoo, and scrub brush. Ren stood quietly when I turned the faucet on and let the cool water run down his legs. As I moved the hose up onto his shoulders and back, he took in a quick, deep breath at the shock of it and then closed his eyes. He rested a back foot, lowered his head, and began smacking his lips as horses do when they are completely at peace and enjoying the moment. I stood on my stepstool to soap his enormous mane and to scrub the top of his back, telling him he was the most wonderful horse ever. He was the biggest horse I had ever washed. He was the biggest *anything* I had ever washed. As soon as I had finished rinsing him and turned the hose off, Ren opened his eyes and his nostrils fluttered. He looked down at the cement, watching the bubbles disappear down the drain. His head moved from side to side, trying to see where the hose had gone. He had enjoyed his bath so much, he wanted another soaking.

Ren was in love with baths. I could have washed that horse all day long and turned him into a truck-sized prune, and he would have been happy. It was such a big job that it took over an hour to bathe him. Time continued to usher us forward, but I was never aware of it during bath time. Sometimes I scrubbed him in silence—just my horse and me. It was a time to marvel at Ren's heavy bone structure and muscles, slippery and cool against my hands. Sometimes I told him all about my life, and always he had one ear flicked back in my direction, listening. Ren learned all about my mom and dad, the pets I'd loved and lost, the jobs I'd had, the people I loved, and those I didn't. He listened when I told him about the men I'd loved—the ones who'd hurt me and the ones I'd hurt. He knew of every ache and pain in my body. He heard me cry at times over the frustration of my ever-increasing hearing loss. He listened to my hopes and dreams without throwing darts to burst them. He listened without reproach when I asked him pertinent and open-ended questions and then answered them myself.

I told him about the things I'd seen as a police officer, things that I'd never told a person. I told him about a little eight-year-old girl I'd interviewed when I was the child abuse investigator. She was a beautiful child with long, dark hair and huge brown eyes. She told me that her uncle had "put his thing into" her and that it had felt "like a monster down there." I asked her if there was anything more she wanted to tell me. She said that her father had done this to her also. Each time I asked what I believed was the last question, she would tell me of yet another time her little body had been violated by adult men or teen-aged boys. When she had finally exhausted her story, there had been six. She was eight years old and had had sex with more men than I had.

Ren heard about my escapades posing as a hooker and working undercover in narcotics and how one night another police officer and I almost shot and killed each other during a huge drug raid because we hadn't been introduced. He didn't know I was a cop, and I didn't know he was a cop. We held our weapons trained on each other, each refusing to "put down the gun" until some inexplicable type of reasoning convinced us that we were both undercover officers. Ren heard about the time I was working in uniform and, during a high-speed chase, the suspect mashed on the brakes in his vehicle forcing my partner, who was driving, to crash into it at over eighty miles per hour. We'd had to be cut out of a patrol car that looked like a smashed accordion. We'd walked away without a scratch.

He listened when I told him about an elderly woman I'd met. She used a wheelchair because she'd lost the use of her legs. With hands all twisted and gnarled, she was an artist and created the most beautiful oil paintings from the visions in her mind. She had completed one of a cool winter scene with lots of snow and pine trees. I bought it and I returned later to purchase another painting from her of mountains covered in snow. I spent part of an afternoon with her and told her that I had horses and that I was planning to buy some of the new hay farmers were currently baling. I gushed on and on about my horses. She said the hay reminded her of her childhood. She told me that when she was thirteen years old she'd been helping her family put up hay. She didn't feel well toward the end of one day and went in the house to lie down. Over the next few days, her health became much worse and she was unconscious for over a week. When she awoke, her mother was there to tell her what had happened.

"Polio," she said. "I've been in a wheelchair ever since that summer. Six decades."

I vividly remembered my thirteenth year. It was the year my life began—when Velvet came. I would compete in horse shows and learn to drive a truck and pull a horse trailer. I would spend the next decades running beside a horse, hopping onto its back and sliding off with ease. One person's joy flows on as another's misery is carried along in unison, like a river and its undercurrent, searching for its place in history.

That summer with Ren, I rediscovered the sweet confidentiality with a horse that I'd shared with Velvet as a teen. In exchange, Ren discovered the near-heaven-like pampering of a bath.

Most horses only tolerate baths. They must consider it undignified, yet a small price to pay in exchange for all of the nice hay and grain we humans so freely give them. Maali and Bonnie made it clear that baths were nothing more than an aggravating infringement upon their time. Each stood in the wash rack with her ears slightly back in disgust. Each sidestepped and squirmed and pretended that the drain was a terrifying, cavernous hole waiting to devour her along with the bubbles. Ren's love for baths was second only to his love for food. On the days I didn't feel like leading the horses into the barn, I allowed them to come in on their own through the opened gates from their paddocks. The Girls always trotted directly into their stalls. Ren jogged in behind them, but made a quick turn to the right and parked himself in the wash rack. He'd look over his shoulder at me when I entered the barn after them, as if to say, "I'm ready for my bath now."

It was that summer that I began to notice partially chewed lumps of hay in the paddock and on the floor in Ren's stall. He was "quidding." This meant that he was no longer able to chew up hay well enough to swallow it. A horse that quids tries to chew hay, but then gives up and spits out a wad of partially chewed stems. His episodes of choking had started to increase, and he had a bloody nose or a discharge from his nose almost every day now. What hay he could manage to swallow passed out undigested. Ren's days of eating the hay that he loved so much were over. I sat in the barn and wept when making this life-changing decision for him because it marked a definite point of downward transition in his days. If he'd lived in the wild and was no longer able to chew up grass, Ren would have slowly starved to death or become an easy target for a predator. But he was my responsibility, and I'd made a promise to take care of him.

This time, instead of taking his hay away with nothing to replace it, I searched for something else that might be suitable. I considered buying a leaf chopper and wondered if it would mulch the hay into smaller, more palatable pieces. Before buying such an expensive machine, I tried cutting some of his hay into bits with scissors. After two hours, ruined scissors, and ten sore fingers, I had a pail of finely chopped hay. I offered the new entrée to Ren. He devoured it in less than three mouthfuls—and immediately choked. Whether I chopped it or a machine chopped it, hay would not work. I'd have to come up with another idea.

Once again, I went to the mill armed with questions. This time, Joel showed me processed *cubes* of hay, sold in fifty-pound bags. I bought the timothy/alfalfa mixed cubes, took them home, and opened the bag to find oblong lumps of green things. They looked like Twinkies, but they had the consistency of cement. If Ren couldn't eat hay, he surely wouldn't be able to chomp into these. The recipe for feeding the hay cubes to aged horses was to soak them in water. So, I half-filled a five-gallon pail with cubes and filled the pail the rest of the way with water. Within about thirty minutes, the hay cubes had softened and swollen to fill the pail with a green, baby food–like mush. I offered this creation to Ren. He sniffed it and wiggled his lips around in it surely thinking, "Smells like hay, sorta looks like hay … but it ain't hay." Then he walked away. I was devastated. Ren was upset again because the younger horses had hay and he didn't. He had eaten his grain just as they had, and he knew the routine—as far as he was concerned, a nice pile of hay followed, not this strange looking slop. I left him again, thinking that I would have to come up with something else for him to eat that would make him think he wasn't being excluded. However, I was out of ideas, and no new ones surfaced. Ren was going to have to learn to be content with only his Equine Senior.

Later in the day, when I went back out to the barn to do chores, Ren whinnied and came jogging up to the fence, his body angled a smidgen to the side as usual. I gasped to see that his white blaze was green from his muzzle clear up to his eyes. Aghast and instantly sick with worry, I couldn't imagine what might have happened to him or what he'd gotten into to turn himself green. Ren was as wriggly as an excited puppy as he trotted past me and went over to his pail. His sideways glance as he jogged by told me to follow him as clearly as a person who motions with his hand, "Come on! Come see what I found!"

I obediently followed Ren over to where he had come to a stop. I leaned over and peered into his pail. It was empty, licked clean. He'd had a grand party by himself and had eaten up all of the hay cube stew, and now he wanted more. Exploding into teary-eyed laughter, I threw my arms around Ren's neck and hugged him. He swiped the sleeve of my pink sweatshirt with his muzzle, leaving behind a large patch of green. At last, we had a solution; Ren would get his Equine Senior twice a day and his soaked green Twinkies after each meal to keep him busy, happy, and as close to having a normal life as possible for a horse at his stage in life. He loved those hay cubes. As soon as he had eaten his grain, he was ready for the green Twinkies and he let me know by nickering or pushing on his stall door with his nose. I knew I needed to get them to him quickly. Every day I would bust out laughing to find his entire face solid green, like a baby who gets strained peas smooshed all over his cheeks, nose, and forehead and hasn't a care that the goop is everywhere. Ren never daintily ate from the top of the hay cubes, working his way down—nope. The only way to do it was to plunge his head straight to the bottom of the bucket and slosh around in it.

Ren enjoyed his food so much that just leading him to his stall or feed tub at mealtimes was enough to jumpstart him into dreamy anticipation. He would close his eyes and chew on imaginary food every step of the way until he actually reached that first bite.

During that year, I began to notice little dings and cuts on Ren's head. They were just superficial scrapes and nothing I figured I'd have to worry about, but they still puzzled me. Occasionally, there were small scrapes on the back of his hocks as well.

Every day, when I cleaned his stall, the bedding was increasingly more soaked. He was urinating much more than he had been and was drinking more water. My veterinarian told me that, because of his age, Ren's bladder control, just like that of an older person, was probably not functioning as well as it used to. He said that, as long as the urine was normal in color and the horse continued to drink adequately, I shouldn't worry. It was merely a change because of his advanced years. My horse was aging, and I had to remind myself of that fact every day. But it stung. I knew time would eventually remember that we'd been passed by and turn an about face.

In "people years," Ren was in his late seventies by this point. The beautiful thing about youth in people is that, while you are young, you never once consider what you can and cannot eat. You don't pay attention to your bodily functions. You don't worry about what your teeth can chew up and what they can't. Your joints work fluidly. If you fall, you jump up and carry on. You don't worry about falling, or about breaking a bone. But along with age comes the realization that we have limitations.

The beautiful thing about youth in a horse is the same fluidity, the same spunk, and the same carefree attitude. The beautiful thing about how a horse ages lies in the eloquent mix of dignity and acceptance for what is "now." Ren had no ability to wish that he could still eat or do what he'd been able to do yesterday. He was never given the voice of complaint. He adjusted to the shifts in his body and lifestyle with grace and humor. It was I who felt sorry for him for the changes that I saw and what I knew was to come.

During summer weekends, I put up a portable fence and let all three horses out together while they ate the tall grass in the front yard of the barn. Since it was close to the road, I felt I needed to watch them in case they managed to get out of the pen. I made myself comfortable in a lawn chair and read or listened to music while they happily grazed. Each horse would come up and visit with me from time to time, sniffing my iced tea and wiggling his or her muzzle on my bare toes, and then return to grazing.

On one such day, while the sun was bright and the blue sky was filled with overstuffed clouds, I sat in my lawn chair watching my horses graze. I glanced up from my book to see Maali shoo Ren away from the section of grass she wanted. He tried to turn away from her swiftly, but his legs didn't move as quickly as he wanted them to, and he fell head first and flipped completely over. It was one of those moments that take place right in front of you, happening so fast that you don't have time to react. I stood up, dropped my glass to the ground, and watched wide-eyed as Ren came crashing down with an earth-shaking thud, lying still for a few seconds before righting himself in preparation to get up. But he didn't jump up like a horse usually does. Instead, as he positioned his massive hindquarters under him and attempted to push off with his hind legs, he took three tries before he got to his feet. As soon as he was up and balanced on all four feet, Ren came tottering over to me, reminding me so much of a little child who runs to his mother to show her some small boo-boo. He wanted to be consoled, and he made little whimpering noises as he tried to tell me all about it. He had only a minor bloody nose, but I hugged him and fussed over him and told him everything was okay. I said, "That bad little girl hurt my baby, didn't she?" Ren melted in the baby talk and the fussing. He rubbed his forehead on my shoulder, nearly knocking me over, and, within moments, returned to the grass.

We had passed yet another milestone. This, too, was bittersweet and brought tears to my eyes. Ren appeared to be regressing mentally.

A foal runs to its mother for protection from the dangers in the world. He seeks her out as the one who can shield him from predators and other horses, from storms, and from loneliness. She is the source of all things good in his life. When a foal is weaned, it relies on the herd for protection and on its own individual ability to defend itself and to flee. If an adult horse is injured or frightened, it bolts freely and easily from the scene. But now, I had become Ren's source of security. This strong, swift-footed creature needed his mommy once again.

After that episode, I frequently called him, the "Baby." If the mares squealed at him, I scolded them, "You be nice to the Baby." The source of the dings and scratches on his face and hocks was now clear; Ren was struggling to rise during the night in his stall and was bumping his head on the walls and scraping his hocks during his attempts to get to his feet. Ren needed to be separated from the mares; he could no longer move fast enough to get away when they acted aggressively toward him. It is a horse's worst fear to be down and vulnerable. It would now be my job to protect Ren because he couldn't defend himself, and I doubt that he ever would have tried. I never once saw his ears pinned in anger or defiance, and never saw him attempt to kick at the mares. He was happy and did his best to live at peace in his world every minute of every day. I put Ren in a private paddock where he could still see and visit with Bonnie and Maali, but he was safe from their selfishness and quick tempers.

One day, as I rounded the corner on my way to the barn, I saw a small, brown car parked beside Ren's paddock. Initially furious that someone was messing with my horse, I got out of my truck and marched up to a slim, gray-haired man who was standing beside Ren.

"Do you come to visit him too?" the man asked when he saw me approach. He was smiling and petting my horse.

"No," I said curtly, "I own him."

The man sharply cast his eyes down and away. He took his hand off Ren's forehead.

"I come to visit with him every day. I hope you don't mind," he said in a lowered, meek voice.

Minding very much, I said, "I guess it's okay, but I don't want you to feed him. He chokes easily. I'm not really fond of anyone being around my horses when I'm not there."

"I'm sorry. I can stop if you want, but I look forward to coming down here every day to visit with him. He comes right up to me," he said, looking up and into Ren's eyes, his face beaming.

I left to go do my chores, muttering to myself, "Darn it all, this isn't a petting zoo. Pretty soon there will be cars lined up and down the road to pet the horses."

As soon as I'd finished cleaning one stall, I heard the little car start and I peeked out of the barn to watch it head down the road. I hoped that the man wouldn't return, but, over the next few weeks, every time I came out to the barn, Ren would be standing in the corner by the road in the same place where I had first seen the man. He was waiting for him. When I called Ren's name, he obediently came to me as usual, and we had our normal day doing the things we always did. Still, it irritated me slightly knowing that he was waiting for this man. Looking back, I see a twinge of jealousy, though I wouldn't have admitted it at the time. Maybe I didn't want Ren to be so happy to see somebody other than me.

I suspected the man was giving Ren apples or some other treat. It was too difficult for me to accept that Ren just wanted to see *him*. I never learned the man's name, but I did get to speak with him one other time.

"He sure is a grand horse," the man said. "He's beautiful. He glistens in the sun, and his eyes have so much wisdom; you can just see it."

I tenderly ran my fingers through Ren's forelock. "He is pretty special. I really love him," I said in a near whisper.

"He's so gentle," the man said as he stroked Ren's wide blaze. Ren relished having two people petting him at the same time, and he seemed to enjoy being in the middle of a conversation.

"Belgians are known for being gentle; really, all draft horses are," I said confidently.

"I'd give anything to own a horse like this. I was so happy when I drove by a few weeks ago and found him."

The words, "found him" struck an ugly nerve deep within me. *You didn't find him,* I thought, but quickly attempted to soften my attitude. I changed the subject.

"Do you live near?" I asked.

"Just down the road," he said. "Staying with relatives. I just had cancer surgery, and they offered to have me stay with them until I recover." He continued to stroke the horse's face, looking into Ren's eyes, with tears in his own.

"I really can't say that I'm going to get better. My doctor said that I don't have much longer to live—maybe two months at the most," he said, his voice trailing off. "But it sure makes my day coming down here to see this guy. We talk."

His words rammed into me like a freight train blasting suddenly through the fog. No intelligible response came to me. I felt as if someone had ripped the planet from under me, and I was the only person left, dangling and exposed.

I never saw the man again after that day. For a while, I surmised he was still coming to visit with Ren, and I just happened to miss him. And then one day, Ren was not in his corner by the road. He was in the center of his paddock gumming a few twigs that he'd found. I was shocked at the sudden and absolute change in Ren's routine. I sat in my truck and studied my horse through misty eyes.

He was doing what mattered most to him at that moment, the sunshine warm on his shoulders. Whatever was going on in the rest of world didn't occur to Ren—yet he had given much to a stranger in need, and to me. For the first time, I saw the true beauty of my horse. He no longer looked like an aged, throwaway gelding. He was exquisitely beautiful by any standard, with rippling muscles, a dappled copper coat, and a voluminous mane that was nearly iridescent in the sunlight.

Though I never learned the truth for certain, I assumed that the man had died. I could only guess. Ren knew. He'd always known and understood. There was finality to the scene that caused me to shiver. Ren never went back to the corner to wait again. I would never have another chance to tell the man that it was okay to pet my horse. Any opportunity to let go of my own insecurities was gone. I'd missed my chance to walk up to the man and shake his hand.

Ren had filled a painfully forsaken chasm between what was left of life and the uncertainties ahead—and he'd done this just by being a horse. He'd cared enough to wait for his friend and to be there every day, without fail. And, hard as it was for me to admit, no apples had been involved. He'd listened, without comment, perhaps when no one else would.

There he was, eating twigs. But he owned and walked within a secret grace that had eluded me.

CHAPTER
Six

I T WAS EARLY FALL when Paul and Ellen told me that they wanted to use their barn for storage. That meant that I'd have to move again. Two hundred bales of hay had just been delivered and stacked in a stall. Now I was faced with finding another barn to rent, plus having to move all that hay myself. Finding stall space and barns to rent was becoming increasingly difficult. I had three horses and one of them was a serious special-needs horse. It was no longer safe for Ren to be in the same paddock with any other horses, so that meant I had to find a place to rent that had stalls and *two* paddocks—one for the two mares and one for Ren.

I made phones calls and drove up and down back roads, knocking on doors and asking if anyone had a barn or stalls to rent. Within a week, I found another barn that would suit our needs. Ren had a stall and a separate paddock, and so did the mares. The distance was miserable. It was a seventeen-mile trip one way to feed my horses. In the morning, I would stop on the way to my job as a legal advocate to do chores. Usually there were curlers still in my hair, covered with a babushka. When I arrived at work, I would change into my work clothes and make myself as presentable as possible, given the situation. Almost on a daily basis, some co-worker would snatch a stalk of hay from my waist-length hair. Sometimes there were even a few stray oats perched on the top of my head. And usually I had green horse slobber on my sleeves. After work, I would change from dress clothes into barn clothes again and make the long trip out to do evening chores.

Even though they had stalls, the horses were much happier outside when the weather was decent. It was *always* Ren's choice to remain outside. He loved getting soaked in the rain, and he loved wearing great mounds of fresh-fallen snow on his rump.

One morning, as I pulled into the driveway in the darkness, the headlights of my truck shone on Ren. He was down, but I didn't think anything was unusual and got breakfast ready for the horses. As I approached with Ren's grain, he sat up on his haunches like a dog. He made several attempts to get up, but he was only able to scoot around and around in pitiful circles. He began to flop about on the ground, frantically trying to get to his feet. But, no matter how hard he tried, he couldn't. I watched, solidly frozen between fear and helplessness. I had never seen anything like that happen. Ren continually heaved his body forward, only to fall back onto his side after every exhausting attempt. I rushed over to him and stared. I didn't know what to do. He was worried and scared, but there was no way I could help a horse that size to his feet all by myself. It's not like picking up a six-pound, arthritic poodle. I ran to the barn and got his halter, slipped it onto his head, and tried with all my might to pull him to his feet, but my attempts were futile. I was out of breath, and the pain from the old torn rotator cuff injury sliced through my shoulder. I could do nothing to help him. I started to cry because Ren was so terrified; his eyes were pleading with me to help him. I had never let him down before, and he couldn't understand why I wasn't fixing this problem for him. I just knew that Ren must have broken a bone somewhere in his body, mostly likely in his hips. I turned and walked away from him; numb with the realization that this was it—this was the time Ren would have to be put down. I'd have to drive seventeen miles home to call my veterinarian, make the necessary arrangements, and drive all the way back.

The short walk from the horse to the gate in the darkness seemed wretchedly long, and my steps were mechanical. I cried and shivered, though it wasn't cold. I thought about how much fun I'd had with Ren and about how many times he'd made me laugh or cry, or tried to make me do both at the same time. I didn't want it to be over, but responsible horse ownership also includes the ultimate, heartbreaking decision to have to end a beloved animal's suffering. I put my hand on the gate to unlatch it, and stopped. Was I imagining a warm puff of breath on my neck? I stopped breathing and slowly inched myself around to find Ren standing right behind me. I threw my arms around him and sobbed into his mane. He pressed his lower jaw against my back. And it was as if John Wayne tenderly said, "Don't cry now, little lady." And then he immediately nuzzled my hands in search of his pail of grain. The incident was already behind him. From the moment he reached me, all that mattered to Ren was the wonderful breakfast waiting for him. My tears turned to quivering, gibberish laughter when I realized that, while Ren was down and struggling, he hadn't been worried because he couldn't get up. He'd been worried because he might miss his breakfast.

I did call my veterinarian that evening to ask his opinion and to find some comfort and reassurance.

"I don't know if this is the time to put him down or not," I said, trying really hard to not let my voice waver.

"Is he eating?" Dr. Jansen asked in his Dutch accent.

"Yes."

"And he is up now?"

"Yes. He was tossing his head and trotting when I left."

"Then the time is not now. The horse will tell you when."

I went back out to the barn that night to check on the horses. I prayed over Ren and placed him in the Lord's care again and asked for guidance. As horrifying as the ordeal had been, my assessment of the situation had been wrong. I thought I *knew*. It's hard to accept that you really don't have control over something. Ren's life was not in my hands.

I made an addition to Ren's feed because of this incident. Dr. Jansen recommended that Ren be started on a drug called butazolodine, or "bute" as horse owners refer to it. It's a painkiller that works for horses the way aspirin or Tylenol works for people. Ren was to get one gram in the morning and another at night. While most horses won't eat medication that isn't disguised, Ren never cared. As long as the bitter tablets were somewhat crushed and mixed in with his feed, he classified them as edible and gobbled them up with glee. The bute made a big difference, and he no longer struggled to rise.

Life with an elderly horse is a constant influx of weighing the good and bad and trying new things. You adopt what works for one day into your routine and discard what doesn't. You have to be willing to keep exploring and trying new ideas and new products. I also had to accurately assess the quality of Ren's life on a daily basis. Secretly, you hope that, when the time comes, a horse will pass peacefully in his sleep, but you know all too well that it seldom happens that way.

I had asked to be able to spend two years with Ren. In October, we passed that two-year allotment of time. I gave him apples, carrots, and a few soft horse cookies to celebrate. My prayer had been answered and my request granted, but how many more days were left? From then on, each moment with Ren became even more special, and I started thanking the Lord at the end of every day that he was still with me. We were on overtime.

The horses were only at that barn for two months. Once again, I grew frustrated and felt the need to move. We moved in December when it was cold and snowy. I had to haul nearly two hundred bales of hay again, all by myself, and stack them at the new place. This barn was *thirty-five* miles from home, one way. The owner offered to give the horses their breakfast in the morning so that I wouldn't have to make two trips, but I still went out every evening to do chores and work with the horses. I spent hours with them, brushing each horse, riding the mares, and sometimes leading Ren around the small indoor arena so that he had something to do. I would get home most nights with the hopes of watching snippets of the late news, but I usually fell asleep within minutes of sitting down.

My animals were getting farther away from me, and now they didn't even seem like my own horses. It was as if they belonged to someone else, and I only got to spend time with them.

At first, this stable was very good for Ren. He had a huge pasture all to himself. But he wanted to be with the mares in their paddock, so he constantly walked the fence line. All day long, he paced the fence, back and forth, back and forth. In so doing, he walked himself right into better health. His movement became more youthful, and his arthritis ceased to bother him. Often, I found him with snow on his sides, proof that he had been lying down, perhaps rolling in the snow—and getting up. I was told that Ren was always standing and ready for his breakfast every morning, but no one knew how long it might have taken him to get himself onto his feet.

Ren became healthier and so much more active that he no longer needed the bute, so I took him off the drug. I even started riding him very lightly. We made only a few passes around the arena, but it felt good to be on the horse again, and it was important to Ren to be useful.

The barn was located in the middle of Amish country, and, every day, on my way to and from the barn, I would see buggies pulled along the roads by slim standardbred horses. Every now and then, I would see a team of Belgians towing equipment and loads in from the fields, heading home.

One day, I drove up behind a six-horse team of Belgians that was maneuvering a huge hay rake. The hitch spanned almost the entire road. The sound of twenty-four heavy shod hooves clattering against the pavement was breathtaking. I drove slowly behind and to the side to watch them. In the distance, a semi tractor and trailer approached from the opposite direction. I pulled onto the shoulder of the road, suspecting that this spelled trouble. I didn't want my vehicle to be in the way of either rig. Whatever was about to happen between them was going to take a large amount of space. I expected the semi driver to keep coming and demand the Amish teamster to yield. After all, big business is transported by eighteen-wheelers, and time is crucial. The Amish driver steadily pressed on; he also had a right to be on the road. The road wasn't wide enough for both vehicles; one would be forced onto the shoulder. As the semi approached, I could hear the engine's roar descending as the driver downshifted, gear by gear. He eased the mammoth vehicle over to the side of the road, came to a stop, and let the Amish rig pass. There can't be too many times that semis yield to anything. They don't have to. The driver could have continued; the sheer size and weight of his vehicle would easily have pushed the Amish driver off the road. Instead, *he* yielded, and it was a most supreme display of respect—perhaps one man's salute to the original "teamster" and the original source of "horsepower." Horsepower is not measured by the ability of just any horse; it is measured by the ability of the *draft*. The Belgians turned into the drive at their farm, and the semi tractor rumbled back onto the road, clambering up to speed, and disappeared into the west. It was difficult for me to get moving again. The entire incident had spanned only moments, but I had just witnessed an unforgettable drama of such significance and purity that it rendered me emotionally crippled. So much in the world has been carried forward by the power of horses. So much in our lives still depends on the foundation that the draft horse has pounded into the turf beneath him.

As spring neared, the property owner said that he didn't want any horses tearing up the pastures, so I had to contain them in smaller paddocks. Considering that Ren was capable of plowing up craters that falling meteors would envy, he was confined to a corral. The small pen didn't work for him; he was frustrated and walked in a tight circle, churning up the clay ground and turning it into ankle-deep muck. If he ever slipped in that mess, he would never be able to get to his feet. Every night I crouched beside him while we were in his stall and cut off great hunks of mud that had stuck to the hair on his lower legs, and every night I went home in tears—this was not the life I wanted for my horse. He was miserable, and there was nothing I could do about it.

Eventually, the owner and I reached an agreement: Ren could be in a different, cement floored paddock by himself. This was not the best footing for him either, but it would get him out of the mud, and he could still be near some other horses. The arrangement worked for a few weeks. Ren always adapted to everything; as long as he got his grain and beloved hay cubes, he was happy.

But then things went from tolerable to horrible. I arrived at the barn one day to find Ren standing in a corner. He wouldn't come to me, and I had to go into his paddock to get him. He was covered in white lather and a cold sweat. He was shaking and disoriented. A few feet away from him stood a gnarled metal gate. I could see that it had been broken through from the other side of Ren's enclosure. Two other horses had smashed through the gate and attacked him, and it had happened only moments before I arrived. Ren was nearly incapacitated, tangled in a web of dread and confusion. He walked stilt-like and spastically as I ushered him to the barn and into his stall. I quickly checked him over. The other horses had bitten and kicked him almost everywhere on his body. My heart nearly split to see that his beautiful, long forelock had been ripped almost completely off. He had bite and kick marks on the top of his head and back, which meant that the other horses had brutally assaulted him while he was down. It was obvious that one of them had intended to kill him.

Nausea rose in my throat as I thought of my sweet old horse, scared and struggling to get up—not to fight back, but to get away. I burst into tears imagining the terror that he had been faced with. I was angry at the situation I was in by not having a place of my own, and ashamed that I hadn't been there to shield him from harm. But there was no time to cry. Ren was going into shock. His breathing was shallow and labored; he was icy cold to the touch, and his pulse was weak. He needed to be blanketed, but I didn't have a blanket at the barn. It was late, dark and cold, and I'd have to drive thirty-five miles home to get a blanket and a bottle of Banamine—a powerful painkiller—before driving the thirty-five miles back to the barn. But I did it, and, when I returned with my supplies, Ren was shivering uncontrollably.

Standing next to him, I could feel his intense tremors in my own chest. I bundled him up in a blanket from my bedroom and tied it around his belly with hay baling twine. I measured out the proper dose of the painkiller and attempted to inject it into his neck muscle, but he was shaking so violently that the needle kept bouncing off of his body. After a few unsuccessful tries, I had to grab the syringe with my fist and stab it in. Next, I began furiously massaging his body until my hands burned from the friction. Ren's head was hanging only inches from the floor, and his eyes were listless. I kept rubbing along his neck, shoulders, and back, gritting my teeth to keep focused and strong. After about a half an hour, the pain medication kicked in; Ren finally started to respond, and his body began to feel a little warmer. His coat was still damp, but it was beginning to get crusty in spots, indicating that he was no longer sweating and that his body was trying to dry. He stopped shaking, but he still looked pitiful and confused, like a little old man who'd just been assaulted in some back alley by thugs. It wasn't until close to midnight that Ren began to perk up and nuzzle around in his feed tub for something to eat—a clear sign that the worst was over. I hugged him, and didn't want to let go. I started to cry again when I shut his stall and closed up the barn, leaving him alone in the dark with his injuries.

I took the next day off from work so that I could spend time with Ren. When I came into the barn, he nickered softly to me. He was standing in the same place he'd been the night before. The blue house blanket was still perfectly in place. He was sore and perhaps had felt so unsafe that he hadn't even tried to lie down. He had eaten his breakfast, and he tenderly accepted the apple I presented to him on my palm. I put my arms under the blanket, and felt that his body was toasty warm. Aside from many minor injuries, he would be okay.

Ren had fifteen swollen areas on his body from kicks. Bruises don't show on a horse's body, but I became aware of each one as I ran my hands over Ren's body and he winced at the sore spots. He had so many bite marks that I stopped trying to count them. Some had continued to bleed throughout the night. I rinsed each with warm water and applied a soothing ointment. Ren, always my perfect companion, was the perfect patient too. He stood still, not tied up and without a halter on, as I went from wound to wound.

The saddest part for me to face was his forelock. It now skimmed just above his eyes in a butchered, blunt cut. Horses do pull parts of their forelocks out at times when they get the hairs caught on a fence post or branch. So, it wasn't that the forelock was gone that was sad; it was facing the harsh reality that there would never be enough time for it to grow back to its original length and fullness.

Within a few days, Ren was feeling like himself—happy and back to his constant search for vittles. And, after a few weeks, the majority of the wounds had healed except for one kick mark that left a permanent scar on his shoulder.

Two weeks later, I realized how close I'd come to losing my beloved friend that night. Leafing through an old issue of a horse magazine, I noticed an article about horses—young horses—dying from shock alone. By now, Ren's heart was the equivalent of an eighty-four-year-old human's. If a young, healthy horse could die from shock, Ren must have been wickedly close.

My elderly pal had experienced near brushes with death, but it seemed that his time still wasn't yet about to run dry. I hoped that there was more for us to do. Ren's life reminded me of a Robert Frost poem that I'd read a long time ago. A few of the lines especially seemed to fit, so I typed them up and thumb-nailed a small, handmade plaque to his stall door.

> *But I have promises to keep,*
> *And miles to go before I sleep …*

Horses are horses, and they do horse things. No one will ever know what prompted the other horses to attack Ren to the extent that they broke through a heavy metal gate to get to him. It's possible that the other gelding felt threatened, but, as sad as it was, the other horses were just being horses. Aside from the scar on his shoulder, Ren completely recovered physically. But, there were other scars that he carried with him. Months later, I had to lead him by the strong young gelding that had attacked him. Even though the horse was fenced and could not get to him, Ren's bladder let go, and the urine just sprayed out of him. He was terrified. Just seeing the horse brought back memories of the assault, and Ren began to tremble and pull on his lead line, wanting to flee. I quickly trotted beside him to the safety of his stall to ease his panic and to comfort him. I desperately wanted to promise him that he would never be harmed again, but I couldn't because I still didn't have my own place and sole control over the care of my horses.

"Please Lord," I asked again that night. "Please let me have a home of my own for my animals." There were three things I asked for about Ren. I wanted him right outside my own window, I wanted him to have a buddy, and I wanted to bury him at home when the time came.

It was my dream to live in my own house, right in the middle of a horse pasture. Little did I know that the winds were churning.

Answers were being sent my way.

CHAPTER
Seven

IN LATE SPRING, THE owners of a thirty-one-year-old quarter horse mare needed to find a new home for their horse, so they gave her to me. I knew that she would be the perfect companion for Ren. Her name was Ruby. The minute she and Ren were turned loose together, they were like an elderly couple that had been married for decades. She, of course, was the boss.

Ren was elated to have his very own pal, especially one who had no more interest in biting and kicking than he did. As they lay side by side, sunning themselves in their paddock, they exuded everything that friendship should be. I called them the "Geriatric Crew." Ren's soft eyes conveyed that he had reached a point of fulfillment; his heart was full, and he was content. His life, as far as he was concerned, was complete.

Ruby was the equivalent of ninety-three in human years, and she was extremely arthritic. Her neck creaked and was so stiff that she could barely move it. She also had arthritis in her back legs.

I began doing physical therapy with her by gently forcing her neck to move from side to side and then up and down, increasing the degrees and repetitions each day. I massaged her neck and back. I changed her feed and put her on joint supplements and that good old standby, bute, twice a day.

Within a few months, I was able to start taking Ruby for short walks down the road. She hadn't been out of the barnyard in years, but soon she was almost prancing beside me as we started out. Her head was always up and her ears pricked forward as she seemed to inspect everything from a distance. The length of our walks gradually increased until we were up to six miles total: three miles out, and three back to the barn. People seemed to enjoy seeing a horse being walked like a dog, and they waved at us from their cars and sometimes stopped to ask if they could pet her. Ruby loved being the center of attention.

When Ruby and I returned to the barn, she would nicker to Ren as if to say, "Honey, I'm home." And every time, without fail, Ren whinnied back to her. She was important to him, and he wanted her to know that.

Ruby was doing so well that I decided to try to ride her. I bought a beautiful, dark brown western saddle for her, and a friend of mine gave me a bridle with silver conchos that looked exquisite on her. Ruby was a deep chocolate color, with a rich auburn mane and tail, and she looked gorgeous in the turquoise saddle pad I bought for her. She was very sway-backed, but my veterinarian said it would be fine to ride her as long as her spine was padded heavily and she didn't seem to be in pain. I bought an egg carton–type foam mattress pad and cut it to fit the shape of her back. I placed a saddle pad on her back, then the piece of foam, then the turquoise pad on top of that. With the three saddle pads piled on her back, she was good to go.

The next dilemma to solve was the tenderness of her feet. Ruby had thin soles, and her feet would get sore when she walked on the gravel roads. So, I bought Easyboots for her. They are rubber shoes that fit over a horse's entire hoof and buckle up the front—they're the equine version of track shoes. You slip them on to work the horse and take them off when you're finished. The Easyboots instantly and miraculously changed Ruby's life. Her feet were pain free, and the boots enabled me to ride her down the dirt roads. Ruby's stride instantly became strong, and covered the ground quickly. It was obvious she felt liberated, and she was determined to enjoy every step.

Ruby had lived so long and had done so many things in her life that I got the impression that she believed she owned the whole world. She never spooked at cars, dogs, tractors, garbage cans, or cows—all of the things that usually cause horses to shy. She had seen it all and owned it all, and, therefore, everything was beneath her dignity. Every ride away from the barn was a chance for her to survey her domain.

She was the matriarch, so steady and sure of herself that I nicknamed her "Queen Ruby."

Ruby was a registered quarter horse, and it was obvious that she had been impeccably trained. Often, she would second-guess me, hoping that I'd ask her to "spin." Horses who work with cattle must learn many maneuvers to get them, their riders, and the cattle they care for safely through a workday. Spinning is just one of them. The horse balances on the inside hind leg and spins in a circle or two … very smoothly. Just a slight fluctuation of my body or a rein against her neck, and she would try to begin the fast, whirling movement. I knew that she couldn't spin anymore, and shouldn't, but her training and obedience were so flawless that Ruby would have tried even though it would most likely have hurt her. In her day, she must have been a smokin' hot horse who responded with only a feather-like touch. She'd been an athlete, a working cow horse, and she wasn't about to let anyone forget it.

Ruby believed whole-heartedly that she'd earned the right to be opinionated. She loved to go out riding so much that, if I took too long tacking her up, she would grow impatient and paw the ground to drive home her point. "Come on, come on, we don't have all day. Let's go!" Ninety-three years old and she couldn't wait to go to work. She was so determined. I suspect that, if she hadn't been tied in the barn, she'd have left without me.

One weekend, my friend Kathy and her husband Tim came to visit. Kathy had been one of my best friends for over thirty-three years. We had met one day when I was fifteen and she was eighteen. She and her mom had been out driving around looking for a stable where they could board Kathy's horse. When her mom saw me, she sent Kathy out into the field where I was riding my mare Velvet and told her, "Go talk to that girl and ask her where she keeps her horse."

Kathy came out into the field, introduced herself, and said that she had just bought her first horse and was trying to find a boarding stable. "Do you know of one?" she asked, and a life-long friendship began.

Fellow horse owners consider it a perfect get-together when the day is spent with horses, so Kathy, Tim, and I piled into their car and drove out to my barn, carrying a bag filled with apples, carrots, and Maali's favorite cookies. We petted and fussed over all four horses and gave them treats, but, instead of heading straight back to my house, we decided to go for a short ride. I bridled Ren, and Tim climbed up onto him bareback. I saddled Ruby for Kathy, and I rode Maali. With the two old horses, we only made a few passes around a big pasture at a walk, but Maali pranced and danced her cute little self a short distance ahead of the Geriatrics.

"If Ruby wants to jog, you can let her, but don't go any faster," I called back over my shoulder. I had never asked Ruby to canter when I rode her because I thought it would be too much strain on her legs and spine. But, my warning was a little too late; Ruby and Kathy whooshed by us at a canter. Kathy circled her off in the distance and came back, still cantering, smiling and laughing so hard that she almost lost her seat.

"I didn't ask her to do that!" she exclaimed. "She just took off!"

To be on a horse's back at a canter is to share in an experience that usually belongs to the horse alone; yet, for reasons we can't discern, they allow us to sail along with them and share in this birthright.

Kathy was elated because her own mare Lady didn't canter. She only trotted faster and faster and refused to break into a canter—a rolling three-beat gait.

"I miss cantering so much," Kathy chimed. "This was wonderful! I will remember Ruby forever for giving me that beautiful canter."

Back in the barn, we brushed the horses and gave them more treats. Tim visited with Ren. The stall door was open, and the horse could hang his head over the stall guard. Ren began his slow, deliberate process of sniffing up and down Tim's body, tousling his hair, and nuzzling him on the shoulder. I noticed that Tim had tears in his eyes.

"I don't know why," he said, "there is just something about him. He's special."

Over time, I'd seen enough of how Ren responded to men to know that he enjoyed their company. He always showed his interest and affection whenever a man was around. Ren loved me, but he was one of the "good ole boys." He was, indeed, just like John Wayne—a "man's man," as someone had once defined The Duke. Even though Ren was a gelding, and a horse, he included himself in the secret and silent camaraderie to which men belong, and any chance for Ren to get together with one of the guys made his day.

Ruby was beautiful. Her legs, although arthritic internally, were clean and straight. Every inch of her sang out that she had excellent breeding. She was beautiful at thirty-one; she must have been breathtaking in her prime. And Ren loved her. He followed her everywhere she went. If Ruby walked two steps forward, Ren walked two steps forward. If Ruby moved to another patch of grass, he was beside her. If she decided to lie down in the sun, he joined her, often lying so close that their bodies pressed up against each other. Ruby never pinned her ears at Ren, and she seemed to enjoy his company as much as he enjoyed hers, yet she wasn't as demonstrative as he was. She was both alluring and mystifying, as a female should be, and she knew precisely how to keep him mesmerized.

Sometimes the two of them would take off as fast they could across the pasture. For Ren, that meant an easy trot because cantering was too difficult for him then and he no longer made the attempt. He'd gracefully allowed that part of his life to slip away. But Ruby cantered, slowly so that she was never more than one stride ahead of her partner. If her arthritic hind leg was bothering her, she'd stick it straight out behind her, like an oar hovering above water as a boat skims along. She'd canter on three legs as if she'd done it that way all her life. Ren and Ruby didn't launch off very often, but, when they honored the urge, it was more exciting than watching thoroughbreds on the track. Though they could no longer gallop, that ancient God-given call to race the wind still beckoned deep within them.

Ruby occasionally experienced bouts of not eating for days in a row, but she always managed to rally, and, after a few days, she would be her feisty, independent self—Queen Ruby—again. One day, however, the look in her eyes was different. It was distant. She had stopped eating again, showing no interest in her food. I sensed that Ruby the matriarch, who knew so much and had carried herself to the age of ninety-three in human years, had made a choice. The same determination she had possessed all of those years to keep going was the same determination I was up against in trying to coax her into living again once she'd resolutely made the opposite choice. She had defied the odds by living such a long life, and she defied me when I tried to help her.

I bought Ruby every kind of horse feed on the market. She refused all of it. I tried sweetening feed with molasses and then with applesauce. I chopped hay with scissors, and soaked different kinds of hay cubes for her, but she wouldn't even look in the buckets I offered. She drank only enough water to satisfy an immediate thirst, and then she stopped drinking altogether. I had been on the phone with my veterinarian daily, and every suggestion he made, I responded with, "I tried that."

In just a few days' time, Ruby dropped a tremendous amount of weight. She was gaunt, and her coat lost its luster. She ceased to urinate. Ruby had made the decision to stop. I could either agree to be included, or she would do it on her own.

I spent one last night with her alone in her stall. I held her sweet face in my arms and told her how wonderful she'd made my life. I told her it was an honor that she had shared time with me this past year and had taught me so much. I thanked her for all of our walks and rides, and, most of all, for being so good to Ren. And in the quiet of that night, I asked her if she wanted to go. Horses have a way of communicating with those of us who listen to the silent language one heart speaks to another. Ruby gave me her answer.

The next day the veterinarian came. He briefly examined her, but he knew, as I did, that the old mare was ready. Good veterinarians do not take this part of their jobs lightly. To put a horse down just because she is old is not reason enough. He needed to have a diagnosis before he could proceed. As he examined her, he found her lymph nodes to be enlarged. Her lungs rattled from fluid, and he assessed that her kidneys had ceased to function. There were no gut sounds in her belly. Her eyes looked as if they no longer belonged to her.

The doctor placed his pencil-sized flashlight into his pocket.

"Her body is shutting down," he said softly.

Together, we escorted The Queen to a soft spot on the grass, and he gave her the two injections that ended her life. It was quick and peaceful. After the veterinarian left, I remained for a while with Ruby.

"Thank you, Lord," I whispered, letting the tears fall. "They don't come any better than this."

Dusk was on the way when I finally went back into the barn. I got my scissors, returned to Ruby, and cut off the bulk of her long tail hairs. It was my plan to save them and bury them someday on my own property so that a part of her would always be with me. But, as difficult as that was, there was yet another task to perform that night.

Many years ago, one of my Arabian mares gave birth to a filly that was weak and didn't thrive. I had to separate them and take the tiny foal to the veterinary hospital at Michigan State University for testing. The results were alarming; the filly had serious congenital faults and had to be euthanized. Though it was agonizingly sad for me, I came home to a frantic mare, drenched in sweat, screaming and searching for her baby.

The four-day-old filly had just vanished from her life. There was no way to explain to Dalyce what had happened, and, because of that, there had been no way to console her. I don't believe she ever gave up the hope that her baby would be coming home. Horses are incapable of blame. I alone saddled myself with the weight of my actions, though there had been no other choice. I made a promise then to all of my future horses, that I would never again put one of them through such an experience. I would allow them to see and sniff their deceased offspring or pasture buddy to give them closure.

As darkness neared, I led Ren from his stall to Ruby's body. When he approached her, he was stoic and calm—he already knew. They'd had their quiet moments in the barn the night before to communicate, but I still gave Ren the opportunity to finalize the situation and see her lying lifeless and still.

Ruby had graced our lives for not quite one year. I once heard a certain woman's personality described as being so expansive that she filled up a room. Ruby's personality was larger than life. She filled every paddock, every road, every day with herself. I loved her. I loved her because she was a horse, and I loved her because she had made it in this world for so long, and knew so much about life. I loved her for all of the secrets she'd stored up, and had taken with her. I loved her because of the gift of laughter and that wonderful canter that she gave to Kathy, my best friend and a two-time breast cancer survivor. But most of all, I loved her because she was good to Ren.

On the night of Ruby's death, Ren did not eat his grain.

CHAPTER
Eight

IN EARLY SUMMER, I started long lining Ren again. This time we went down the roads. Ren was happy to get out of the barnyard again even though we only went our usual mile out and mile back. As healthy and robust as Ren had become, I wondered if he might be able to pull a cart, providing that I could locate one that was not too heavy for him and that was reasonably priced.

I had come to know a number of Amish people. My farrier for Ren was Amish, and the man from whom I bought feed for the mares was Amish. So, I contacted some of the Amish horsemen to see if such a draft horse cart existed. They all told me to get in touch with a man named Marvin and gave me directions to his farm.

Marvin, an older man with twinkling blue eyes and a mischievous grin, shook my hand when I met him in the driveway to his home. He impressed me right away as someone who knew everything about driving draft horses, and we became friends immediately.

"I have a really old Belgian gelding that is the love of my life, and he's doing so well right now that I think he can pull a cart. It would give him something to do, and I've dreamt of driving my own draft horse, as long as I can find a cart that's not too heavy and not too expensive. I was told you had a cart for sale," I blubbered, barely taking a breath.

"Yes," Marvin said calmly. "I think I have a cart you might be interested in."

We walked across the road to a storage barn where the cart was kept. I had never seen a cart quite like this one. It was homemade, mostly of steel, painted green and white, and it had two bus tires and a bus seat big enough for three people. It was perfect.

"What will you sell it for?" I asked excitedly.

"I will sell it to you for two hundred and fifty dollars," Marvin said with a grin that looked more Irish than Amish.

"That's all? Is there anything wrong with it?"

"No, I used it a lot, but I don't have a horse right now that fits it."

"I want it," I said. "Do you know where I can get a harness?"

"I will throw in a harness for you too," Marvin said.

Marvin had taken up great delight in helping this amusing English woman assemble yet another one of her dreams. It must have been entertaining for him to meet someone who was so giddy over something that was so mundane to him. After all, driving horses had been his way of life from the moment he was born.

My new Amish friend was a harness maker and dealer, quick and knowledgeable. We walked back across the road and into his harness shop. This was a *real* harness shop. It smelled of leather and dye, and there were dozens of huge draft horse harnesses hung on racks. Marvin also made driving wear for the light buggy horses, but the draft harnesses were his specialty. Within minutes he had pieced together various leather parts so that they formed a complete harness. It was old and cracked, but still "safe and usable," Marvin said. A large pile of weathered, used collars was heaped on the cement floor, and Marvin selected one.

"This one should fit him," he said, and he hung the collar over my outstretched arms. I got goose bumps. It was heavy and settled on my arms like it was supposed to have been there all of my life.

"I've never harnessed a draft horse. I don't even know if *he* knows what to do," I said haltingly.

"How 'bout I come down in two weeks, hitch him, and we'll go for a drive?" Marvin offered.

"That would be fantastic," I squealed.

Marvin shook his head, trying not to look too amused. But he chuckled anyway and said, "I'll have someone bring the cart to your barn tomorrow."

I was so excited about the cart coming that I couldn't sleep that night. I had flashbacks of all those old nights before shows when I was a kid. I was a much bigger kid now, but the excitement was exactly the same. The event was made all the better because it was a Friday night, and I didn't have to work the next day.

I drove to the barn first thing in the morning and spent my time pacing back and forth in the isle in between cleaning stalls and peeking out the barn door every two minutes in hopes of seeing the cart arrive. Around noon, a truck pulled into the driveway with the cart strapped onto a flatbed trailer. Two men jumped out of the truck, unbuckled the straps and ties, and rolled the cart down onto the pavement, and ... away they went. The cart had been deposited in less than two minutes, and there it was: my cart, my own draft horse cart, parked right in front of me. I was a wee bit intimidated. After so many years involved in nearly every aspect of horsemanship, I was facing something completely new. I went over to the cart and touched the tires and then the long poles that hold the horse in place, called shafts. I climbed in and sat in my cart, folded my arms across my chest, grinning, and said out loud, "Awesome!"

"Ren should at least get to see his cart," I rationalized, so I brought him out to the barnyard where the cart was parked. It has been said that horses cannot show emotion in their faces, but for those of us who love them, we know how very wrong that nasty assumption is. As soon as Ren saw the cart, his eyes got larger. His ears popped forward and his nostrils flared. He knew what it was, and he approached it almost as if I weren't with him—the way you excitedly, yet tentatively, walk up to an old friend you haven't seen in years. I held onto the lead rope and let him take me along, back into his youth. Ren touched the cart with his nose and looked at me as if to ask, "For me? It's for me?"

Ren eagerly examined every inch of that cart, wiggling his muzzle all over it. He reminded me of elephants when they caress each other or when they tenderly run their trunks over the bones of other elephants that have died. I have never seen a horse do this. It was no different than one of those times when you find a box of your old toys in the attic. Perhaps hidden beneath some yellow newspaper is that favorite doll, truck, or maybe a song flute from grade school. You pick up the doll and hold it close to you. Alone, when you find the box containing the toys, you have those moments where it's just you and the past; your chance to escape back into days gone by, into times you had forgotten until you found this old friend. So it was for Ren; he was alone with that cart and alone with his memories.

After his inspection was complete, Ren turned his attention once again to me. I didn't think it would be asking too much too soon to at least try to back him into the shafts, just to see if he would be manageable. Ren marched backward into the shafts as if I had been asking him to do it for years. I let him stand between them for a few minutes. He looked at his left side and at his right side, checking it all out. I had never seen him look so tall, so exuberant. It was as if he was beaming, "It fits! Look at me!"

Ren hesitated when I asked him to walk out of the shafts. His back hollowed, and his head sunk down. Indeed, he was disappointed that we weren't actually going to go somewhere.

"You probably aren't even broke to it," I teased as I led him back to his stall.

Two weeks was a long time to wait for Marvin to come help me. Daily, the cart stared at me and beckoned. But, eventually, the time passed, and, on a cool fall Saturday, a driver brought Marvin to the barn. Heavy blue-gray rain clouds threatened overhead, but Marvin still came, prepared to help me hitch my horse. I had brushed Ren and he was waiting, tied up in the isle of the barn.

"I think it's been at least a decade since he was hitched," I said after shaking Marvin's hand and exchanging some small talk that was boring and getting in the way of my plans.

"He'll be fine. He didn't forget," Marvin said. He looked at Ren, gave him a quick pat on the shoulder, and got right to work by rearranging the harness that I'd hung over a stall gate. Marvin lifted the heavy collar up onto the horse's neck and then hoisted the harness onto Ren's back in stages even though it was all connected.

"Tighten the belly band up about this much, see?" Marvin said, looking sideways up at me with his hand between the horse and the leather to demonstrate the correct tightness.

I nodded.

"The britchin, it rests here," he said.

Marvin explained each piece of the harness, its purpose, and how it should be adjusted. I wanted to gallop around, bucking and squealing like one of my happy horses because I was so excited. But, difficult as it was, I also knew I had to maintain a professional demeanor and not become too goofy.

Marvin slipped the bit into Ren's mouth, eased the bridle onto his head, and adjusted it to fit.

"The overcheck is just about right for him. It hooks here," he said as he clipped the overcheck in place. "The overcheck is a strap that keeps the horse from putting his head down too far," Marvin said. It all looked so easy.

I let Marvin lead Ren out to the cart, and I followed just off to the side and behind. *My horse* was all dressed up in work clothes—*real* work clothes. The tug chains made a faint "ching" as Ren strode out of the barn, the hames (the two metal brackets that fit into grooves in the collar) listing from side to side with each step. He looked professional; the black harness and bridle with the blinders made him look like a real draft horse.

"Your horse is all business," Marvin said after he'd backed Ren into the shafts and began the process of hitching the cart. When the Amish say that a horse is "all business," it's a lofty compliment to the horse and to its training. I couldn't have been more proud if my son had just been handed an Olympic medal.

"I'd hook the tugs on the last link for him, just like this," Marvin said as he attached the heavy chain to the cart.

I nodded again.

"Do you know what this piece does?" Marvin asked, raising his eyebrow and lifting a smaller strap in his hand for me to see.

"No."

"This is a hold back strap; there's one on each side. They keep the cart from ramming into him when you stop."

"Do the reins go through these loops?" I asked, trying to sound knowledgeable.

"Lines," Marvin corrected. "They aren't reins. They're lines. And, yes, that's where they run."

Marvin got in the cart. "Get in," he said.

My body hesitated, but, since my heart was already in that cart, I climbed in too.

Once we were settled on the seat, Marvin clucked to Ren, and the horse moved off immediately. At that point, I could no longer contain nor conceal a tooth-filled grin and big, liberating guffaw.

"My horse!" I exclaimed. "My horse is pulling a cart!"

It was Marvin's turn to bust out laughing. We'd traveled less than fifteen feet.

Marvin's confident hands guided Ren out of the barnyard and down the lane to the large pasture.

"How is he doing?" I asked.

"He's good broke," Marvin said in the jargon the Amish use to describe a well-trained horse. "He knows all about it, and his manners are impeccable."

I was about to burst, but I somehow managed to stifle my giddiness. Every now and then, Marvin looked at me and tried not to laugh, but it was almost impossible for him.

"You're going to sit there and grin this whole ride, aren't you?"

"I can't help it, Marvin; this has been a dream of mine since I was a kid."

The cart rolled along smoothly, even over lumps and bumps in the grass, and the bus seat was as comfortable as any easy chair. We circled the pasture twice and then Marvin asked Ren to reverse. Ren daintily stepped with his left front leg, crossed over with his right front leg, step by step until he had pivoted the cart almost on the spot to go in the opposite direction. I had only seen horses do this maneuver at the draft horse show at Michigan State University.

"He knows how to do *that*?" I asked, wide-eyed.

"I told you he didn't forget," Marvin said. "Now it's your turn to take up the lines."

My eyes flashed at Marvin. "Nah," I said, backing off. "I don't think I'm ready to do this, not yet anyway. You can drive."

"He'll be fine. You're ready," he said. "I thought this was your dream."

"Don't we have to change places?" I asked.

"No, just take up the lines right where you are," Marvin said.

"Maybe I need you to practice with him a few more times before I do it," I suggested in a soft voice.

"Then I guess we'll sit out here in the pasture all night because I'm not driving him back," Marvin said as he set the lines down on the dashboard and folded his arms across his chest. I almost expected him to start whistling.

I took up the lines. The heavy, thick leather felt good in my hands, like when you're grasping a steering wheel for the first time, and feeling that restrained power reverberating through your arms.

"Just cluck to him or tap him with the lines," Marvin said. I did, and Ren stepped off.

"I'm driving!" I hooted.

There I was, forty-eight years old, sitting beside an Amish man in a cart, learning to drive a draft horse for the first time and giggling like a teenager.

"This is driver's education, Amish style," I exclaimed.

"Start turning him," Marvin said. "Take the lines up a little shorter; ask him to turn just like you do when you ride. Give and take … give and take," Marvin said. "That's good; now don't hit that rock."

"I'm driving! I'm driving my own draft horse!" I blurted.

At that exclamation, Marvin looked away, but I knew he was laughing.

After we'd traveled around the pasture twice, Marvin said, "Now let's turn around again and go the other way."

I brought Ren to a halt and asked him to begin turning to go in the opposite direction. Once again, he gracefully executed the tight pivot and turned us completely around. I hadn't a clue what I was doing.

"Drive him back up the lane," Marvin said. "This is enough for him for one day, and it's enough for you too. You're about to fly out of this cart. Don't hit that fence post on your way. Remember, you can't see around these big guys; you can't see anything in front of you because he's wide and the cart sits low, and, remember, the wheels stick out to the side quite a bit."

Once back in the barnyard, Ren waited patiently to be unhitched. I put him in his stall and went out with Marvin to wait for his driver to arrive. My lack of confidence and finesse must have been quite apparent because Marvin offered to come again and give me another lesson, "in a few weeks," he said. I agreed, but had an inkling that I wouldn't be able to wait for him to return to try it again.

As soon as Marvin left, I dashed back to Ren. A different horse greeted me at the stall door. He stood taller, pumped up, and very, very proud of himself. I hugged him. It was always fun to hug Ren because my arms didn't fit all the way around his shoulders and neck; this big, fluffy teddy bear was a lot of horse to hug.

"You know more about this than I'll ever know," I gushed.

I tried to make myself wait for Marvin to return, but I just couldn't do it. I felt like a little kid who has been told to wait to ride his brand new bike until Mom or Dad was around to help him, while all the while the bike sits tantalizingly within reach. I eschewed the logic and the wait, and, the next day, I was back in the barn with the cart, the harness in my hands and the horse waiting patiently in the isle.

The harness was an antique and, along with the collar, it all weighed in at over a hundred pounds. It was huge and extremely cumbersome to maneuver. But, if I wanted to drive my horse, I'd have to figure out a way to get that monstrosity onto him. My stepstool had steps that were spaced exactly right for me to be able to go up one step at a time with the harness completely covering me, looking like some science fiction sea creature. The first few tries, the harness ended up in a very large mass of tangled leather on the ground, completely unrecognizable. Imagine about one hundred pounds of tangled Christmas lights in a heap at your feet. My guess is that this is how one learns the parts of the harness and where they fit. The first time I actually got the harness onto Ren's back, I was proud of myself as I stepped back to view my accomplishment. My shoulders collapsed with a sigh when I realized what I'd done. "I don't believe this," I said to myself. The entire harness was inside out. I had to slide it off Ren's body and try to figure out which side was which before trying it again. During all of this, Ren remained motionless.

The first piece I had to get on him was the collar. It weighed forty pounds. The weight of a draft horse collar is an issue, but, even more of an issue, is the shape of it and the fact that, somehow, you have to get that hunk of odd-shaped leather over your horse's head and fitted down onto his shoulders. For some, it's easier to present the collar, get the horse's face and head through it and then slide it down. However, this is not so easy if you are five foot two. I unbuckled the collar, opened it, and thrust it up and around his neck from below. The stiffness of the collar held it in place just long enough for me to scamper up the stepstool and fasten the buckle at Ren's withers before it fell off. Next, I put his bridle on. Ren was very good about accepting the bit, but I still had to stand on the stepstool to reach the top of his head to adjust it. After several clumsy attempts at towing the harness around and stepping on most of the leather straps, I invented my own way to lug it where it needed to go. I looped the hames over my left arm and ran my right arm through the bellyband and rump safe. Then I stepped through the tugs, the heavy straps and chains that actually pull the cart, and walked with a portion of the harness dragging behind me. I was completely covered in harness parts.

The stepstool had to be placed perfectly. If it was a mere fraction off as I began to climb the first step, I had to back myself down the step and reposition it. Most horses would eventually start to fidget in hopes of not being harnessed, but Ren never did. Through all my trials and foibles, he stood still, waiting for me to figure it all out, waiting for the day I would finally have a routine that worked for us.

It took three failed attempts with the harness draped over me to discover that, if I stood on the first step of the stool, I could heave the hames over Ren's withers and that would free me of one-third of the bulky contraption. I would then climb up onto the second step and hoist the back band onto his back, and then the rump safe and the britchin would follow. The hames had to be raised and pulled up onto the collar and fit into the grooves and buckled near the horse's chest. I had to get off the stool and move it farther down the length of Ren to adjust the back straps, then climb back up and continue the process until the harness was settled. Next, the off side of the harness had to be adjusted as well, using the same process of climbing up and down the stool and moving it along the horse for each section of the harness. Lastly, I attached the lines to the bit, and we were finally ready to go to the cart. Even though the harnessing left me huffing and puffing like a weight lifter, I quickly forgot about that the moment I saw the cart.

Some horses fuss and refuse to back into the shafts, or they won't stand still once they are in because they know that if they do stand, the tugs will be fastened, and they will have to go to work. Walking forward one inch can be just enough of a distance so the tugs don't reach to attach to the cart. Some horses require more than one person to hitch them—one to stand at the head and prevent the horse from fussing and another person to finish the hitching. I thought back and remembered the bay mare named Queenie that my father had owned, and I just knew that she'd practiced every avoidance technique until it was executed with expert guile. But Ren was a sweet, understanding horse, and I was able to hitch him by myself every time. There is no doubt that, in his many years as a pulling horse, he too had discovered all of the tactics to avoid working, but I always knew that Ren *chose* to stand for me. During hitching, there are a few minutes when the horse is completely loose while you are back at the cart attaching the tugs. The horse could bolt or walk out of the shafts and go wherever he wanted. A horse can also create problems by turning sideways in the shafts before you have the other side hooked, but, once again, Ren stood like a stone as I went back and forth from one side of the cart to the other, fastening, making adjustments, and then double-checking to make sure that I'd done everything correctly. He waited calmly until I was seated in the cart and ready to go.

For about a week, we drove around the big pasture in the safe confines of a fence. I have often looked back and thought what a sight it must have been for those passing by to see one lone woman in a cart being pulled by a draft horse all by herself and laughing. I'm sure people wondered why I had chosen to drive in a fenced pasture in lieu of going down the road.

After a week or so of practice, I drove up to see Marvin—in my truck—and reported our progress. He was pleased, and we both agreed that he didn't need to come back to my barn.

It wasn't too long after that the roads out into the real world became irresistibly enticing. It was a scary venture, but, if I was going to truly enjoy driving Ren, we'd have to get out there. "Tomorrow," I said. And when tomorrow came, I got Ren brushed, harnessed, and hitched as usual, but instead of heading down the lane to the pasture, we went down the driveway. Ren stopped obediently to wait for cars to pass. Millions of fluttery things cavorted in the pit of my stomach. This was a first for me, but it was not a first for Ren.

My plan was to drive down the pavement and make a right turn onto the first dirt road about a quarter of a mile away. Once on the pavement, I still felt queasy about being in real traffic, so I asked Ren to trot. I wanted to get to the safety of that dirt road quickly before we encountered any traffic moving at the much faster speed we'd surely find on the paved road. Ren picked up speed, his hooves clipping along on the pavement in the cadenced, two-beat gait.

I was still jittery, but also beginning to feel a wee bit cocky as we breezed along. Driving my horse was easy. I started to relax and settle in for the ride, but, off in the distance, darkness was approaching. It was a semi truck and trailer, barreling straight toward us. I closed my eyes, immediately sick to my stomach with fear. I didn't know what Ren would do. Many horses are fine in traffic, but some never do adjust to vehicles rushing toward them or passing them from behind. The blinders on a driving horse's bridle help, but the horse is still able to see. Some horses spook at noises, and others spook at something as tiny as a butterfly. Even though Ren had been well trained, it had been over a decade since he'd pulled anything; certainly he could be rusty in traffic. We would never have time to turn around in the road and make it back to the driveway before the truck reached us, so there was nothing else to do but keep going straight ahead.

"Lord, help us," I said, crushing my eyes closed again.

Scenes of a spooked and crazed horse crashing into the ditch with a mangled cart flopping behind him flashed in my mind.

Ren's ears locked forward. He saw the truck coming.

"It's okay, boy, it's just a truck," I cooed.

Ren cocked an ear back to me, acknowledging my voice.

My body stiffened. I held my breath and closed my eyes again as the truck passed at top speed, hurling wind, stones, and dust at us in its wake.

Ren never broke stride.

All of the air I'd been holding inside of me gusted out in one blast. I was emotionally scrambled, caught on shards of both terror and exhilaration.

"Good boy!" I gushed. "I am so proud of you!"

Happy to still be alive and with the scare behind me, I guided Ren to that first dirt road, and we finished our drive. But I'd received a hearty dish of humble pie. I had been the one who needed reassurance; Ren was in charge and had taken care of me.

That first day, when we headed back and the barn was in sight, Ren let out a magnificent, lilting whinny. The great steed was announcing that he had returned.

Ren's neck was tightly arched, his ears forward, and he was prancing. It gave me goose bumps just to feel the power I contained in my hands. I had been given the privilege, for a few fleeting moments, to see what Ren must have been like in his youth, and he was gorgeous. Ren had no concept that he'd gone only two miles, but he knew that he had accomplished something wonderful and something that mattered. He was important again, and he wanted the world to know it.

From that day forward, we were on our own in the driving world, out of the confines of a fenced area and free to go where we wanted. Ren was so easy to drive. I just pointed him in one direction, and he stayed on course. It was like being on autopilot. These trips were near celestial experiences; the roads that stretched ahead of us were tunnels into child-like adventures that we alone traversed. They are some of my most cherished memories with Ren. Just me and my horse with the sun warm on my face. Sometimes wind swirled around us, and occasionally we'd start out with only cloudy weather and come home in a downpour. But they were always special times.

Throughout my life, I have never had a true hobby or something that I have done for sheer enjoyment because most activities I took up would become so much more. Driving Ren was the one thing I did purely for fun. We weren't heading out to win a ribbon; we weren't competing against anyone. There was no clock, and there was no mental strain, just good physical effort for both of us. It was deeply gratifying to be able to harness Ren myself, and then we were free to go, sharing something that we each enjoyed in ways we couldn't communicate to each other and for which there was no need to communicate. Sometimes I sang; sometimes I talked to Ren; sometimes I closed my eyes and just listened to his soft hoof beats on the dirt road. Sometimes I just was.

And it was enough.

CHAPTER
Nine

"**D**ID YOU KNOW YOU have a horse that's down and bleeding?" A woman's shaky voice asked over the phone.

She said she had driven by the barn and saw a lot of blood in the paddock. "That big horse is lying down," she said, "and bleeding."

"Thank you," I stammered, my voice trailing off as the receiver was on its way to the base of the phone. I stumbled around like a nearly knocked-out prizefighter as I looked for my gloves, boots, and my knit cap. Once thrown together, I grabbed my coat on the run, bounded into my truck, and drove to the barn. I had no idea what catastrophe would greet me. Had Ren impaled himself on a fence post? Had he broken a leg or ruptured an artery? The drive to the barn seemed no less daunting than driving through downtown Chicago blindfolded. If I'd driven one hundred miles per hour, it still wouldn't have gotten me there fast enough. As I pulled into the driveway of the barn, Ren was standing by the back fence. I parked my truck and left the door ajar so as not to startle him, and cautiously opened the gates to get into his paddock. There was blood everywhere, made even more alarming against the white snow. The ground looked like a slaughterhouse floor.

Ren nickered and heartily marched through the snow to join me. He wasn't limping. He didn't look sick, and didn't appear to be injured. I walked all around the horse, examining his legs, poking and prodding his body, and listening to belly sounds on both sides. I peered at his undercarriage, pinched along his spine for signs of pain, felt his throat and examined his eyes, and found no obvious reason for the grotesque scene.

Dumbfounded, and with my hands on my hips, I stepped back and stared at him. According to Ren, this was all a silly waste of precious time that would be better spent devouring half a dozen apples. He rubbed his muzzle on my coat sleeve, sniffing for treats, and left behind large smears of drying blood. He'd had a nosebleed, and it must have been a pretty bad one. Closer inspection of the paddock provided a few clues that helped to solve the puzzle. A flake or two of loose, unruly hay had tumbled over from another corral and had come to rest within Ren's reach. He must have been overjoyed at his sudden and unexpected windfall as he gleefully jammed the course—and dangerous—fodder into his mouth. Trying to swallow, he'd pierced his throat and nasal passages, but had continued to search for more wayward hay, blowing his nose to clear the blood and blasting bright red patches at every stop he made. When the woman who called me had driven by and seen Ren lying down, she was observing only his afternoon siesta, nothing more.

Once Ren was in his stall munching on his apples and grain, I went back out to the paddock with a shovel to rearrange fresh snow over the blood so that more passersby wouldn't become alarmed at the sight. I also wanted to make sure that I hadn't missed something more serious. More worrisome than the blood was discovering the spot where Ren had been lying to relax in the winter sun. The area had been flattened and the snow smoothed under his generous weight as expected, but the space was much larger than it should have been and there were many deep hoofprints gouged into the packed snow. The shovel slipped from my hands as I stared at the evidence. It was obvious that Ren had been struggling to get to his feet again. Sometimes it's so easy to forget that, with all of its related health issues, age is not reversible. During the times that Ren was doing well, I casually flung to the side thoughts of losing him—like yesterday's socks. But each time he slipped into the trenches was a gruff reminder to me that his overall health was diminishing. The reminder always struck me rudely and when I least expected it.

The problems that Ren encountered trying to get to his feet had increased. He also had developed an unusual manner of shifting his weight on his legs by slightly elevating one front leg, placing it back on the ground and then lifting the other front leg. Sometimes he shifted his weight from one back leg to the other as well. It was peculiar, but not something that stood out as a major complication at the time. Both Ren and I adapted to the changes in his body and lifestyle. He'd discovered a way to get to his feet, all by himself, and I forced myself to refrain from trying to help. Once I grew accustomed to seeing him down and making attempts to get up, it became easier to accept that Ren was never again going to jump up like a young horse. If I didn't watch and didn't rush over to him, he'd eventually figure it out and muscle to his feet. Sometimes it took as long as fifteen minutes. There was nothing I could do to help him anyway, and watching only seemed to make it worse for him because he felt pressured to stand. Ren problem solved by learning to get to his feet in stages; he would wait calmly in the sitting dog position for a few minutes before attempting to hoist his hind end up. Then he would rest in between each attempt. He would usually be successful after two or three tries. Occasionally, I provided a little incentive by placing his beloved black feed tub within his view. The mere sight of that tub and the anticipation of the grain it held would have propelled Ren to his feet if he'd had four broken legs. With his eyes locked on the tub, his body never failed to follow along in that direction, like a snow-bound car being pulled out of a ditch by a wrecker.

So many times I would ask myself why he continually chose to get down on the ground if it was so difficult for him to rise. But are people any different? We know that we shouldn't lie out in the sun too much, but we just can't resist those golden rays. They feel too good to pass up and we do it anyway. We know we shouldn't smoke or overeat, but we do. Whether it was in the snow or in the warm summer sunshine, Ren enjoyed the times he could lie down. The soft sand of an indoor arena is also marvelously delightful for a horse to roll in, and Ren couldn't resist that either. It seemed as if great magnets pulled him down onto the sand each time he was turned loose in the arena while I cleaned his stall. The mere thought of scratching his sides and back on the sand was so great a temptation that it obliterated any memory that the old horse might have had about the difficulty that would follow. I always kept an eye on him and was frequently able to distract him with a treat so that he wouldn't try to roll. When his knees started to buckle, I would race into the arena calling, "Ren, treat!" And that was usually enough to dissuade him. Once he had an apple or a carrot, he'd forget what he'd intended to do and hang around at the gate hoping for more treats. But there were times when I wasn't quick enough. If he really wanted to get down onto that sand, he was quite cagey as he pretended to sniff at a pebble or a leaf, all the while keenly aware of my location, like a little kid waiting to swipe a cookie before supper. He'd quickly drop to his knees and plop down onto the sand with a resounding plunk. Although he could no longer actually roll from side to side, Ren was content to lie on the cool sand for a moment, scratch his one side a little and call it good.

"Lord, please get him up," I'd say as I left the barn with a loaded wheelbarrow, headed out to the manure pile. I'd return to the barn never sure of what I'd find. But, every time, Ren would be standing at the gate.

As winter eased into spring, there were yet more changes and difficulties to face that seemed to appear almost overnight and then quickly escalate. Ren started losing weight rapidly. I increased his grain and hay cubes, but his weight continued to plummet; he was suddenly and wickedly drifting away. The loss was so dramatic and so sudden that, within just two weeks' time, no one but I would have known it was the same horse. Within one month, he'd lost all muscle tone. Each vertebra protruded from his spine. His ribs stuck out like knife blades, and his hip bones jutted out freakishly, like those of a starved Holstein cow. What little flesh he did have on his body hung loose like limp drapes, and it felt blubbery like a squishy, under-filled waterbed. Yet he still had a voracious appetite.

Within three months, Ren had lost five hundred pounds. He was gaunt, sunken, and dissolving right before my eyes. The veterinarians whom I had spoken with were inclined to assess that the condition was age related and surmised that Ren was nearing death. Each one reminded me that my horse had passed the usual life expectancy of most horses and had far exceeded the years allotted to draft horses. Even so, I had been frantically searching the Internet for anything similar to Ren's condition, any source of information that might help. But I also knew that it was not fair to let him starve to death either. Even though he ate everything I put in front of him, it was obvious that any nutrients, proteins, and fats weren't being absorbed or utilized by his body. Feeding him was like dumping food into a bottomless cistern. I was desperate and knew time was rapidly dwindling.

Everything changed one day as I sat at my computer in what surely were my last futile attempts to find anything that might help my horse.

I typed "muscle atrophy in draft horses" and, suddenly, help burst onto the screen as miraculously as trucks loaded with supplies slide into a war-torn refugee camp. A veterinarian by the name of Dr. Beth Valentine had been at the forefront in discovering and researching a metabolic condition called equine polysaccharide storage myopathy, more commonly known as EPSM. Belgians were the first breed listed as predisposed to the condition.

Trembling with excitement at this revelation, I devoured the many articles posted on the site. All of the articles stated that EPSM had frequently been the cause of severe muscle wasting and weakness. Affected horses experience massive muscle and weight loss in the back, shoulders, and hindquarters—and have great difficulty rising. It also described telltale symptoms where the horse shifts its weight from one leg to the other, and Ren had been shifting his body weight in that manner for several months. He had all of the classic symptoms. The research indicated that horses with EPSM are unable to derive adequate energy from carbohydrates, which are found in grains and the sweet feed that most horses are fed. Horses affected with EPSM might not show any signs of the disorder until late in life, and frequently it wasn't noticeable for years. Most often, when the signs do appear, they are attributed to conditions such as arthritis, neurological problems, and a host of other gait and age-related maladies. Horses can have arthritis or other medical issues *and* EPSM, which can further confuse and delay diagnosis and proper treatment.

Dr. Valentine's suggested and proven treatment involved replacing those carbohydrates with a type of fat as the primary source of energy for the horse. She also provided a list of the feeds that are acceptable for EPSM horses. Equine Senior was on the list.

It was that simple. I was ecstatic to find some answers, but worried that I hadn't found the information in time to help Ren. *Please, please, let there be time,* I prayed. All I'd have to do was add two cups of vegetable or corn oil per one thousand pounds of Ren's weight to his feed—four cups of oil per day. The intent is to train the muscles to draw energy from fat. If the treatment appeared to be successful, Ren would have to consume the oil for the rest of his life. I shut my computer down, left home immediately, and bought a five-gallon jug of corn oil.

Two cups of the corn oil mixed in nicely with the Equine Senior. The other two cups I slopped on me and dribbled on the floor, but I managed to pour enough over the soaked hay cubes. Ren watched me intently while I mixed his supper, and waited patiently for me to serve it to him. The articles had stated that some finicky horses need to have the oil added to their feed gradually over a period of days and possibly weeks. But of course that didn't apply to Ren. He gobbled up both slimy messes without hesitation and continued to do so, meal after meal.

After just one week, the results were astonishing. In that short time frame, Ren had gained enough weight back that it was noticeable. He began to fill out in his belly and haunches, and his coat became shiny again. Day by day, new muscle was forming too. I could hardly wait to place the weight tape over Ren's withers every day, reach under his belly and pull the tape around to reveal the daily increase in pounds. It was as exciting as opening a Christmas present.

The new diet saved Ren's life. It was miraculous. In all of my years and experiences with horses, I had never witnessed such a profound weight loss, especially when the horse had maintained normal eating. I'd rescued many starved horses, but they had been emaciated from months of neglect. I had never seen such atrophy of the heavy muscles in the hindquarters, shoulder, and back either. Within a few months, Ren was healthy again. He was stronger and more beautiful than he'd ever been.

Throughout Ren's recuperation with EPSM, he hadn't been out in the cart. In fact, during those precarious months, I'd forgotten about driving entirely. But Ren had recovered so successfully that he began pacing around in his paddock and tossing his head. He was bored and ready to get back to his job. It was like having a new horse all over again. At least we'd been given another allotment of time. I didn't want to waste it, and sensed that Ren didn't want to either.

I hadn't even peeked at the cart in many months, so when I pulled the tarp off of it, I suddenly realized that it really was kind of ugly. When I had purchased it, I'd been so excited that it never occurred to me then that the bright color was a bit garish.

Three ninety-seven-cent cans of spray paint from Wal-Mart were all it took to transform the cart from shocking kelly green to navy blue. But the best part was finding two brand-new, chrome hubcaps at a resale shop that fit the bus wheels.

I had been out driving on the freeway one day and saw a sign advertising hubcaps for sale. I had to go to the next exit and head back the other direction, exit the freeway again and drive for what seemed like the length of the Great Wall of China before I found the place. Thousands upon thousands of chrome and plastic hubcaps of every size and style were mounted outside and inside of a dilapidated building. I'd never seen so many hubcaps in my life. I didn't know this many hubcaps existed. The owner of the business, a red-haired, tattoo-covered young man who said his name was TJ, proudly said he had hubcaps to fit any vehicle "in the universe." There were so many hubcaps that it was overwhelming and just about impossible for me to choose two. The selection was narrowed down to not much more than four thousand when I told TJ that the wheels had previously been on a bus. TJ went to a back room and returned with six different hubcaps.

"What do you think of these?" He asked.

In that batch, I found the perfect hubcaps. I bought two.

Once I had them at the barn, I had to pound them on with a sledgehammer because the wheels were so old and the rims had dings and bends. (I'll never be able to get them off.) But once on, they sure did look sweet.

When we went for our first drive down the road after Ren had recovered, we went in style. Ren proudly pulled our elegant, navy blue cart with its tan bus seat. The shiny new hubcaps sparkled in the sunlight.

The months we'd just passed through had been harrowing and difficult, and, once again, Ren had survived an ordeal that probably should have killed him.

There were more to come.

CHAPTER
Ten

HORSE AUCTIONS HAVE NEVER appealed to me, and I'd never attended one. Many of the horses are sold for slaughter. Up to one hundred thousand American horses have been slaughtered every year for decades. Their meat is shipped overseas to several foreign countries to be consumed as a delicacy. For a while, people assumed that the horses sold for meat were just the skinny, old rejects and were chopped up for dog food, but horsemeat is no longer an ingredient in dog food. Occasionally, old, severely neglected horses find their way to a slaughterhouse, but most hauled to this grim fate are healthy and young. Since there is a surplus of horses in this country, there is no need to purchase the skinny, neglected horses when so many fat ones go through the sales. Foals are slaughtered right along with their mothers. Beloved companions and riding horses that were stolen, or, in some other manner, ended up getting misplaced along the way, go to their deaths too. Some auctions have become dumping places for unwanted horses. Many horse owners who dump their animals at those types of auctions without trying to find decent homes for them know exactly what goes on, and they are not exempt from their responsibility as pet owners. Blaming the buyers and the slaughterhouses exclusively for their gruesome work is unfair, as the horse's death is the end result of the decision a horse owner made to start the process. In America, horses are considered companion animals, not food animals.

I didn't think I could attend an auction without hurting someone or without bringing home every horse tagged for the kill trucks. But one day, as I was driving past the local fairgrounds, I noticed many horses of various breeds and sizes all over the place. There were buggy horses, draft horses, and riding horses everywhere. It wasn't a horse show because no riders were competing in the ring. A large sign at the entrance said that it was the Henry Auction. This time, I stopped.

With trepidation in my boots, I entered the first barn. Horses were whinnying, and I could hear the auctioneer's voice rattling over the loudspeaker. This was a serious horse auction. Approximately one hundred Amish men and women sat in the bleachers and stood ringside. They were there to purchase their next "vehicle." There were just as many non-Amish people standing ringside in hopes of purchasing a nice riding horse. Outside of the sale barn, there were vendors set up to sell horse tack, equipment, and feed.

I was pleasantly surprised. The sale ring was clean and bright with fresh sawdust, and the majority of the horses were in good shape. The prices they were bringing indicated that they were most likely going to real homes.

I watched the actual sale process for a while and then spun my way through the biggest barn. As I came around a corner, I saw a golden dappled palomino tied in a stall. The gelding far out-classed any horse on the premises and brought me to a sliding stop.

"What on earth are you doing at an auction?" I asked out loud as I stepped into his stall to stroke his neck. The words had erupted out of shock to see such a horse at an auction and not so much that I actually expected an answer.

He was one of the most beautiful horses that I had ever seen in my life—if not *the* most beautiful. He was tall—at least sixteen hands—with flawless, straight legs and a muscular body, perfect for dressage. His eyes were deep pools of navy blue that instantly revealed the highest level of intelligence. He was furiously pawing and had managed to dig a hole about two feet deep in the sand at the front of his stall. He was angry. Perhaps angry that he'd been taken there, left and confined just like an ordinary horse. He was no ordinary horse, and he knew it. It would be like locking the president of the United States in a closet and then forgetting about him.

I fell in love with this palomino gelding the moment I laid my eyes on him. If I had been able to design and custom order the horse of my dreams, this was it. But I had to think with my head and not with my heart. The timing was all wrong for me to buy another horse. I was renting expensive stall space for the horses I already had and driving that terrible distance to care for them. I sat in the bleachers trying to wash the lump in my throat down with Diet Coke as I watched the gelding go through the sale ring. A "catch rider," someone who rides horses in the sale ring for their owners, rode him, and he was visibly irritated with her. She jerked on the reins, jabbing his mouth with the bit. His ears were flat against his head, and he angrily wrenched his tail from side to side in protest barely withholding some serious bucking. The gelding sold for a fairly high price. I hated to see him sold at all, but at least he'd brought enough money to keep him safe from slaughter. Even so, I learned that a horse dealer had purchased him anyway, and I was heartsick. Sometimes a dealer will bid on a horse and then run the same horse back through the ring to be sold again in hopes of getting a higher price. That's exactly what happened. I knew I had to stay and see this through to the end. As the horse was led out of the arena for the second time, I prayed for him, told the Lord I wanted the horse more than anything, but I knew it wasn't a wise thing to do. I asked the Lord to watch over the horse. I let go and left.

In the middle of winter, I started seeing a large pickup truck that always pulled an aluminum livestock trailer. On the driver's door of the truck there was a decal that read, Gordon's Hauling. Everywhere I went, I'd see the Gordon rig. If I went to the feed mill, the truck would be parked in the lot. If I stopped at a stop sign, the truck would cross in front of me. If I drove by one of the Amish farms, I'd see the truck rolling down the driveway. These unusual events went on for several weeks. I had a strange feeling that I was supposed to contact this man, but I wasn't quite sure what to say if I did get in touch with him.

In the meantime, another friend of mine, Carol, had called to let me know she was looking for a horse for someone who lived near her, and she wanted me to keep my eyes and ears open if I saw or heard of one that might be suitable.

I had met Carol two decades ago when she called me about a horse I had for sale. She came out to see a beautiful black Arabian mare that was priced at $15,000, but fell in love with a darling part-Arabian gray mare, and she bought her instead—for $500. I still kept seeing the Gordon truck everywhere I went, and, with Carol's horse search on my mind, at least I had a reason to contact the man. He wasn't listed in the phone book, but, after making a few calls to some other horse people, I had his number. His name was Mike. I called him later that day.

"I'm not sure why I'm calling you," I said. "I see your truck everywhere, like it means something … like I'm supposed to get in touch with you."

There was a long pause, and then Mike spoke. "Well, I'm a horse dealer and I haul horses too. Are you looking for a horse to buy?"

"No, not really," I said. "I guess I am looking for a horse for a friend's friend, though. What have you got?"

Mike said that one of his Amish clients had a pinto horse for sale and that it was going to be sent to an auction if someone didn't buy it within the next week. Mike gave me directions to the farm, and we agreed to meet there the following day.

A sign at the edge of the driveway to the farm said, Henry Auction Service. Mike pulled in right behind me and, as we walked toward a pasture, he explained that he was very good friends with Jacob Henry, who owned the auction company. Mike hauled many horses for him to and from farms and various auctions.

When we entered the pasture, three horses came walking toward us. Two of them were bays.

"See those spots on that gelding?" Mike stated as he pointed to a tall, lighter-colored horse.

"That's not a pinto," I exploded. "That's a palomino. Those are *dapples*, not spots. He's a dappled palomino. This is the horse that was at the auction! I'm crazy in love with this horse!"

Mike, an experienced horseman, looked a little sheepish and chuckled, "I *thought* they were some kind of spots." He explained that this gelding was indeed the very same horse that had gone through the auction twice. It had been five months. Jacob had purchased the horse for himself the second time the gelding went to the block.

"But he's not quite what Jacob wanted," Mike said. "He wanted a horse he could ride when he's hunting coyotes, but the horse doesn't care too much for that."

The horse's name was Tom. Tom is certainly a nice name for a man, but the name fit this horse about as well as a crown fits a stump. The palomino came close to me, yet remained a short distance out of my reach. The horse had such presence that it was almost like I should have curtsied before him. I bought him on the spot. He was meant to be my horse, and I wasn't going to take the chance of losing him again. Too many strange things had happened to lead me back to him. If I hadn't taken the chance and called Mike, I would never have known that my dream horse had been stashed away for me so close to home and that he was for sale again. I had experienced such a feeling of urgency when I'd seen Mike's truck over and over. The trail of events was made all the more compelling when Mike told me that Jacob was planning to take Tom to another auction in just two days. If I'd ignored those urges and strange coincidences, I would have never known that my prayer had been answered and that the horse would be mine. By this time, I had some extra cash, and adding another horse to my clan wasn't impossible or foolish.

Jacob, a kind, dark-haired man in his thirties, had taken excellent care of the horse and had truly hoped Tom would be suitable for what he wanted. But it hadn't worked out that way.

"Then I thought he might be a good horse for my wife to ride, but she says he's too tall," Jacob said. "So he's gotta go. We don't keep horses that don't fit our needs."

Jacob brought the horse into the barn isle to saddle him so that I could see how he did while being ridden. Tom stood quietly while the western saddle was placed on his back and cinched up. He accepted the bit and calmly walked back into the barnyard with Jacob. The horse appeared to be very well broke. Jacob put his foot in the stirrup and swung up. The very moment Jacob eased his body down onto the saddle, Tom exploded. The horse gave no warning as he launched straight up with all four feet off of the ground. It was as if Jacob had been fired from a canon. He rocketed air-born a good two feet and returned to earth like a lump of dirt. The horse bolted away in a gold streak and raced around a distant pasture. Mike and I rushed over to Jacob, who was slowly beginning to stand. He wasn't injured. I looked over my shoulder to where the horse was galloping in circles with his tail rolled up over his back and his neck arched. He was snorting like a wild stallion. He was magnificent.

"He's never done that," Jacob said, shaking his head and smacking the dust off his trousers. His straw hat was about fifteen feet away. Mike grabbed that and handed it to Jacob.

"You don't have to take him," Jacob offered apologetically. "I would never sell a bad horse to anyone. Really, he's never bucked."

I believed Jacob. Even though he was a horse dealer, it is not the Amish way to lie. But it didn't matter if the palomino never bucked, or if he acted like a bronco every minute of his life, it was a done deal. It didn't matter if he was a dangerous rogue. He was going to be my horse.

Jacob and I went out to the pasture to try to get him. But the horse continued to race around full tilt. He'd stop every now and then to snort and stomp his front feet as wild horses do to scare predators away.

Jacob shook his head. "Man, that's a good looking horse," he said.

"Let me try," I said. Jacob backed away and headed toward the barn.

The golden horse held his head high over his shoulders as he cautiously allowed me to move a few steps closer to him. I spoke softly and kept taking small strides in his direction. The horse didn't turn away from me, but he made no attempt to approach me either. I kept inching closer. He stopped snorting at me and he finally lowered his head. His eyes softened. He'd made a decision. I was accepted.

I reached the horse's shoulder and stood quietly beside him so as not to spook him. I gently took hold of the dangling reins. The horse walked back to the barn beside me without further incident.

Unlike Ren, this horse did not greet everyone with immediate acceptance and unquestioned joy. He was aloof and made it clear that you had to earn his affection if you were to get it at all. He chose who he allowed into his life: who he allowed to touch him, who he permitted to get on his back. But he immediately gave his heart and his will over to me. There was nothing I couldn't do then—and cannot do now—with that horse.

That first day after I approached him in Jacob's pasture, being with this horse was like being in the presence of royalty. I changed Tom's name to Prince. Prince is a "one-man horse," and I wouldn't even think of letting someone else try to ride him. He might permit it, but, if he didn't, the resulting consequences might be far too serious to even take the chance.

Prince is the leader of the herd. While bossy horses usually challenge and stake their claim by squealing, kicking, and biting until the previous top dog is toppled, Prince, instead, works magic with the other horses. He has such self-assurance and confidence that he oozes charisma. It never even enters the minds of any of the other horses to question his authority. He is a brilliant, yet compassionate leader. Usually, when new horses are added to a herd, they all go through rearranging themselves into an appropriate pecking order. There are squabbles, squeals, kicks, and a few bites bestowed until everything has settled and peace is restored. Every time a new horse is introduced to the herd, Prince is the first to greet it. He is so charismatic, so sure of himself, that there is never any question about who he is. The other horses and the new horse will resort to sorting things out between them, and the usual fracas ensues. Prince intervenes every single time. He will allow them to meet and scream at each other for just a few minutes, and then he moves in to calm things down. But he does this without ever making a sound, without a kick, and without a bite. I have witnessed that horse slide his large body between two horses who want to fight. Most of the time, all he has to do is just start walking in the direction of a potential tiff, and the combatants scatter. He is able to do this without ever placing a mark on any horse. He is a natural-born leader. When a storm is approaching, Prince gathers his herd, and, by some unspoken, quiet method of communication, he convinces them to huddle and remain in the spot he has chosen for them.

One day, a fox was trotting across the hayfield. Prince immediately rounded up the other horses and placed them all in a closely packed configuration. Then he trotted out to the far corner of the pasture, snorting and stomping. Though it was just a fox and not a serious threat, instinct told him to protect his herd, placing himself in harm's way for their sake.

"I wish he could be the president," I told Carol once. "I'd vote for him in a flash. He's the best leader."

Carol likes to compare horses to celebrities, and we have a lot of fun thinking of appropriate famous people who fit a particular horse. Her favorite mare, Sienna, is a beautiful, dark Arabian mare. She calls her Elizabeth Taylor.

It's been said that we horse folk are all a little strange. We aren't too concerned about the accusation because we're a happy, innocent lot. We groom our horses, stick a mane comb in our hair to keep it handy, forget that it's there, and go to the store. We show up for work with hay chaff stuck to the back of a dressy sweater, and we are clueless as to how peculiar it might look to others when our fingernails are stained shiny black. It's hoof polish—doesn't everyone know that?

Once, when I was sitting in the bleachers at the United States Arabian National Horse Show in Louisville, gabbing with a small group of friends, we somehow got on the subject of horse poop. "Horse poop doesn't smell bad," someone said. "Everything about horses smells good." "Horse sweat and leather …"

About that time, other folks sitting near us were snared. Horse people cannot resist this type of chitchat. In fact, starting a conversation about horse poop is a great way to meet others just like you. Start talking about it, and you will separate the real horse people from the "I've always wanted a horse" sect. Non-horse people stare wide-eyed, wrinkle their noses, and then they go golfing. The true horse folk delve right in.

Those of us sitting in the bleachers that day didn't need much more than an hour or two to successfully analyze and rate the aromatic essence of cow poop, pig poop, and dog poop. And, as one person from California pointed out, and to which we all unanimously agreed, "Chicken poop, in large quantities, is without doubt, the worst."

So, it made perfect sense to me when Carol said, "Prince is Bill Clinton." Even though we had a good laugh, she had nailed it, square on.

Whether we like Bill Clinton or not, there are some things we cannot deny: he's tall, suave, debonair, and charismatic. Most importantly, there was never any question over who was in charge when he was the president.

"The Royal One," or "Mr. President," as he is frequently called, took one aged Belgian draft horse under his gilded and all-powerful, protective wings. Right from day one, Prince understood that Ren needed someone to look out for him. He immediately knew that Ren could not and would not defend himself. He knew he was the underdog and that simply would not be tolerated in Prince's herd. The other horses had supreme respect for Prince, but they didn't buddy up to him. They behaved as if he truly was royalty, like the big boss who's always there to supervise but you just don't feel worthy of approaching unless he seeks you out first. Ren had the exclusive honor of being close to Prince. When one of the mares would pin her ears at Ren and start to head for him, Prince would nonchalantly place his body between Ren and the grumpy little mare. That was enough to deter any forthcoming scuffle. Only Ren was allowed to scratch his chin on Prince's withers. Only Ren was allowed to graze from the same patch of grass as Prince and to drink water *with* him.

And then there were four.

CHAPTER
Eleven

It was just a ramshackle house in the middle of an overgrown field on fourteen acres of land. The place appeared deserted, although signs of a previous life were strewn about. The tangled yard was peppered with various old and rusty car parts, black garbage bags, and haphazardly sized pieces of rotting boards. Behind the house, a makeshift shed stood tilting and ready to fall over. Straw poking its way out of the small structure hinted that goats or sheep had recently lived there. Partially rolled and twisted sections of livestock fencing bulged up like sparse and jagged stubble from the weeds and brush. Even so, the land brought tears to my eyes.

Straight to the south, a vast, flat field gave subtle glimpses of prior glory. Amid the wildness that had overtaken the field, random stalks of timothy and alfalfa dared to continue fighting for a place to breathe.

I closed my eyes and envisioned a grand horse barn with an indoor riding arena. I pictured the land elegantly sectioned off with white vinyl fencing. *My horses would be so happy here,* I thought. But it would take monumental work to bring the property and the house back to life. There was no fencing. There was no barn. It was just a house in a field, and both were in extreme need of repair.

I looked in the real estate booklet and wrote down the name and phone number of the agent who had listed the property. For several years, I'd been thumbing through the real estate guides every time a new one was published, with the same attitude one thumbs through the Sears catalog as a wish book. My hopes were dashed against the rocks when the agent told me that the place had just been taken off the market due to legal issues. "I can't even show it to you," he said. "Not now, not ever, because it's been permanently taken off the market. Apparently the seller is going to live there now."

"It would have been perfect for me," I told another best friend Nancy, a real estate agent, later that night when we spoke on the phone.

"Maybe it will be listed again," she said hopefully, knowing how badly I wanted a place of my own.

I had met Nancy and her husband Tom twenty-five years ago when I was a state trooper. I had been transferred from the west side of the state to work in narcotics out of the Lansing area. I needed a place to board my horses, and ended up boarding at the same stable where Nancy and Tom kept their horses. We were the only two boarders at this very private facility, and, since we both had Arabian horses, we immediately became friends. Nancy and Tom were newlyweds, and, within a short time, they were able to purchase their own house and land, complete with fencing and a barn. They invited me to keep my horses at their new home, so I joined them. We've been best friends for over two decades.

For a few weeks, I drove by the house on Townlane Road at least once a week, just checking to see if the for sale sign might miraculously appear again. But it didn't.

Never one to face a closed door without trying to finagle it open, I woke up one morning thinking that maybe the owners of the property would like to hear from someone who would be interested in purchasing it, if they ever *did* decide to sell. I knocked on a neighbor's door and was told that the owner's name was Guy. Another neighbor gave me his phone number and told me that he lived only one mile away from the property I was interested in. I called him. He said he was still considering selling the place, but wasn't quite ready to make that decision yet. He took my name and phone number and said he would let me know, "in a few weeks."

Days stretched into two weeks, and I hadn't heard anything from Guy. I didn't want to lose hope, and I kept praying, but it was beginning to seem like it just wasn't meant to be. And then one day, Guy called.

"I want to sell the place to you," he said.

Guy suggested we meet. Later that day, I finally got to see my place.

"Don't you want to see the house?" Guy asked.

"No," I said, "the land is more important."

We walked the perimeter of the field. Even though there was more junk way out in the field, it was still beautiful. I was able to envision where the barn and fencing would go. It was like finding a starved horse and seeing beyond the matted mane and ribs to the real beauty waiting to emerge beneath the signs of neglect.

Finally, we went into the house. It would need a lot of work. Guy had just put all new windows and exterior doors on the house. The windows were large and let lots of sunlight in. I glanced out the kitchen window out into the field and could truly envision that big gray barn, fencing, and my horses romping happily.

This was my first home purchase, and the paperwork and the waiting between each step of the process appeared mountainous. You visit the property and wait, call the bank and wait, meet with the appraiser and wait. Wait, wait, and wait. Nancy kept reassuring me that this was normal and the nature of real estate deals. But I wanted it all to happen immediately.

Guy gave me a set of keys to the house even though we were far from closing on the venture. I went there every night after work and painted. Since the house was totally empty, painting was easy. I could slop onto the sub floors to my heart's content. Though I still didn't own the house, I felt that, if I painted it, it would just become mine in some magical manner.

Guy is a fairly short, slightly rounded man in his mid seventies. He had been in business all of his life and frequently purchased land and then resold it. He owned many rental properties, also. His wife Joyce is approximately ten years younger than he is, and she is a beautiful lady. Age hasn't diminished her joy in being a woman, as is evident by her carefully styled hair and artistically painted fingernails. She loves good perfume and wears her makeup perfectly so that it complements without competing with her looks. Guy and Joyce became like second parents to me. They were inspired to help me achieve my dream to have my own home for my horses. They offered to carry the mortgage for three years. They also paid for new carpeting, of my choosing, throughout the house.

Weeks before the closing, I started moving some of my belongings into the house. I did this more to stake my hopeful claim than because of any real need to move. Plenty of stories circulated about real estate sales falling apart, even right at the closing, but that didn't stop me. I had already fallen in love with the place and would have been devastated beyond measure if I had lost if for any reason. But the closing went through without issue. On a bright July morning, the keys were officially handed over to me, and the property legally became mine.

I hired a man to build a shed row barn for the horses and to put up fencing for two separate paddocks, one for the mares and Prince, and the other for Ren. Once again, I had to wait. Waiting for the barn to be built and fence to be erected before the horses could come home was even more grueling than waiting for the closing. But finally, the day came.

Mike Gordon hauled the horses home. All four settled in immediately and peacefully. The rolled in the dirt—their very own dirt at their very own home—and they seemed to know that we would never be moving again. Each horse had a separate stall in the barn, yet the gates were always open so that they could come and go as they chose.

My joy soared beyond the end of the sky. Everyone who has had a passion, some dream or goal held so close that it becomes reality, understands. The big dream had come true. Every few minutes I would look out the window, see my beloved horses contentedly munching on grass, and start to cry. Then I would laugh and then cry some more. My kitchen window is large, and I can stand at the sink while I'm washing dishes and watch my horses.

That first night, I even got out of bed to look out into the moonlit paddocks to make sure they were still there and that it wasn't just a dream.

In the morning when I awoke to do chores, I bounded out of bed and peeked out my bedroom window. And there they were—my horses. I went out through the garage and called Maali's name. She jumped and stared at me as if to ask, "Where did you come from?" Maali had always been very sensitive to the sound of my vehicle. Barn owners often told me that they knew when I was coming because Maali would start whinnying the minute she heard my truck, long before I actually pulled into the driveway. Then she would trot along the fence when she saw my vehicle because she was so happy to see me. But on the first morning at our home, I had surprised her, and she was a little embarrassed that she hadn't detected my arrival by the sound of my truck. She seemed shocked that I had managed to pull a fast one on her. But by the time nightfall came, all four horses realized that I lived there too.

In the evening, I left my bedroom window open and allowed the sweet scent of the field drift into my room. From my bed, all I had to do was turn my face to the right, and I could see the horses milling around in the paddock. Those first beautiful, warm summer mornings began with me calling out to the horses through the window screen. Within two days, they had learned to stand huddled in the corner of their paddock that was closest to my bedroom, waiting to hear my voice. When I said good morning to them, they all whinnied and paced anxiously for me to get out there and feed them breakfast. By the third day, it was apparent that they'd had some type of meeting and had come up with a plan. They would all assemble in the corner of the paddock that was closest to my bedroom at approximately six in the morning and wait like guards for the moment that the curtain moved. Then they would all start snorting and nickering, not waiting for me to speak. Eventually, they even learned to watch for the bedroom light to come on.

Nancy and Tom came up frequently, and we worked hard fixing my home. In ninety-five degree heat, Nancy and I stood shoulder to shoulder and pounded thirty support stakes into the ground with a sledgehammer to set up a temporary riding ring so that I could work with the horses. We peeled off wallpaper and borders and we painted; we put up curtains and drapes; we weed-whacked; we cleaned, fixed, and repaired.

That first summer, I hauled truckload after truckload of junk to the dump. There were car parts, fence parts, bottles, rubber mats, refrigerator parts, and rope half-buried all over the property. There were several areas that had been used as burning sites, and I spent hours on my hands and knees scooping up nails and shards of glass. Every time I walked in the field, I'd find yet more half-buried junk. In increments, everything began to shape up.

I put up my portable fencing again and allowed all four horses into the backyard to mow the lawn. All I had to do was open up the back door and I was with my horses. Maali tried several times to follow me up the two cement steps that lead into the kitchen. If I had been several decades younger, I would have let her come in.

My dogs, a basset named George and a sheltie mix named Callie, finally got to see what all the fuss was with these creatures that took up so much of my time. The closest they had ever been to the horses in the past had been sniffing my jeans and trying to discern the peculiar smell of horses. Now, they could see them, and Callie took great pleasure in barking when the horses got to playing and bucking. She decided it was her job to let me know what they were up to. When I opened up the back door, George would yodel and bay when he saw the horses. He'd wag his tail as if welcoming them into his world. "Yes, those are your horses, Georgie," I'd tell him.

I hung a birdfeeder in the backyard and enjoyed watching various brown-colored birds grabbing their meals throughout the day. One day, Callie alerted me that "they"—the horses—were up to something. She barked and fussed until she convinced me to look out the kitchen window. There was Ren, batting the bird feeder around with his muzzle, pummeling it as if it were a punching bag, trying to get at those tasty seeds. I opened the backdoor and said, "Hey, fella, what do you think you're doing?" Ren looked at me quickly and briefly, only to be reasonably polite, and then he returned to his mission of trying to master the birdfeeder. He worked on the flimsy plastic for about three hours, and, by evening, he'd discovered a reliable manner of whacking the now-disheveled-looking plastic container from the bottom, causing a mere thimbleful of seeds to leap out and onto the ground. He'd quickly drop his head to the ground and gobble up the well-earned fruits of his efforts and then thump the feeder with his muzzle again. At the end of the day, the bird feeder was scattered in bits all over the ground. Ren had punched that feeder so that it finally cracked like a piñata, spilling its goods entirely.

I replaced that feeder with a goldfinch feeder once I noticed that there were three sets of the little songbirds sitting on the edge of the roof at the back of the house. They would look down at me quizzically, as if inquiring when supper would be served. Each brilliant yellow bird sat right beside his more olive-colored little "wife," and all six of them lined up along the roof. When the finch feeder was finally hung, they dove for it, fluttering their wings to ward off the purple finch family that tried hourly to intrude.

There were other birds that I hoped would come: bluebirds, hummingbirds, and chickadees. Most of all, I wanted killdeers.

I had noticed my first killdeers years ago when I was a trooper. I was cruising out of the parking lot in a patrol car and saw a bird scurry across the pavement in front of me. A bunch of teeny, perfectly round little balls of fluff whirled along after her. They looked like a handful of ping pong balls that had been scattered across the driveway. The baby birds were running so fast and so smoothly that they seemed to be rolling. I got out of the car and went in search of the little balls. They had vanished from my sight. But the mother was limping and dragging a broken wing. I followed her, wondering what could have happened in that short amount of time to have injured her. As soon as I was snared, she straightened her body, flew a short distance away and then resumed her broken wing charade. I'd been had. But I was hooked on the birds from then on, though I never knew how to attract them. They build their nests in such bizarre places: on the sides of the road, on golf courses, in driveways. They seem zealously independent and downright stubborn. It's always amazed me that they don't get run over or have their nests smashed before the baby birds are able to flee. I had a driveway and open fields now, but no killdeers ever selected those places to build their nests.

Eventually, I fenced my front, back, and side yards into beautiful pastures with white vinyl posts and rails. I was finally living in the middle of a horse pasture. My home is perfect for me. I have only three miles to drive to my office, and that means I can come home for lunch to let the dogs out and to check on the horses. All four of the horses learned very quickly what time to expect me, and Maali would be waiting to hear even the faintest sound of my truck. As soon as I pulled in the driveway, she'd begin nickering and letting me know that she would like a few of her cookies. They all wanted lunchtime treats, but they had decided to let Maali to do the talking for them, since she'd proven herself so adept at it.

Once the additional fencing was up, Ren had the entire back pasture all to himself, and he patrolled it as steadfastly as if he were a cop walking a beat. He was on the move constantly, and his hoofprints covered every inch of the turf. Sometimes, when I came home for lunch, he would be happily grazing. Sometimes he would be standing under the shade of his massive elm tree, resting a hind foot and dozing. He'd take a few deep breaths and perk up when he heard Maali announcing my arrival and then he, too, would come over to the fence to get his treat. Usually John Wayne sidled over to me, taking his good old sweet time, but occasionally, if he was far out in the pasture, he'd toss his head the moment he heard my voice and break into a slow, easy canter, ears up and eyes focused on me and nickering as if to say, "Wait, don't go! I'm coming. I'm coming!" It was both thrilling and saddening to see him move with such determination and urgency. He earnestly believed that he was closing the distance between us swiftly and that his feeble gallop was full speed. By this time, there weren't many treats that Ren could chew, but he'd come flying, as best he could, just to be with me.

Sometimes, when I came home for lunch, Ren would be lying flat out in the sun. I wouldn't close my truck door and would creep into the house as silently as possible, so as not to disturb him. "The Baby's sleeping," I'd say to the dogs on their way out to go potty as we went out the side door instead of the backdoor. "We don't want to wake him up." If Ren was sleeping soundly, he wouldn't even arouse when I tiptoed out to give the younger horses their treats. Sometimes, when he was that deep in sleep, I used my binoculars to look for the rise and fall of his ribs to make sure he was breathing.

That first summer, a farmer named Fred agreed to try to cut and bale up the stubble in the field. We ended up with four hundred bales of scruffy hay, which we split. But that was two hundred bales of hay that I wouldn't have to buy that year. Seeing three hay wagons loaded with hay from my own field was an added blessing that I had never asked for.

Fred said the ground was extremely rough to drive the tractor over, so we decided to plow the whole field up, seed it, and begin anew. I purchased the seed, and Fred did the plowing and seeding.

There are certain summer days when the sun is nearing sleep, yet is still radiant, and everything beneath it is golden and almost glowing. If there is a strong, warm breeze passing through it all, I've named these days the Golden Swirlies. Ever since I was a little girl, I have always felt that the wind belonged to me and that it carried special messages if I listened closely and with all my heart. It was on one such Golden Swirly that I took a white plastic bag from a closet. I carried the bag with me and walked out into my freshly plowed hayfield. The rich, brown earth had opened and was inviting in the resplendency the sun had bestowed. Once I was out standing on the soft, warm earth, I reached into the bag and unfurled the long auburn skein. As if the wind had been longing to take her, small strands of Ruby's tail quickly slipped through my fingers as I lifted them and they were whisked away. Some were taken to places unknown, and still others settled lightly in the new furrows at my feet. The next day, Fred came to disk the field. The furrows were turned and smoothed over.

Ruby was forever a part of home.

CHAPTER
Twelve

IN THE MIDDLE OF a steamy, hot night in August, Callie awakened me with the serious, shrill yip that she held in reserve to warn me that the horses were, according to her, "up to no good." She refused to hush, insisting that I not only listen to her, but get out of bed and look out the window. Dense as Callie might have me labeled, I did as she urged me to do.

"I don't see anything, Callie," I told her. But I also knew the dog well, and she never awoke in the night. Her soft brown eyes were pulsing with immediacy. She wagged her black-and-white plume of a tail while still making faint yipping sounds, demanding that I do *something*. As a herding dog, it was Callie's job and innate passion to keep watch over livestock. She kept track of their every movement. Callie trotted over to the door. I followed her and opened it. Everything looked normal. I was just about to close the door when, out of the corner of my eye, I caught a glimpse of a familiar large object. I craned my neck out the door and to the side. Ren was standing in the backyard almost out of sight at the side of the house. He made a friendly good morning chortling sound.

"How did you get out?" I squeaked, not yet having found my voice and not waiting for an answer. I closed the door, patted Callie on the head, who was presently smirking, "I told you so. Next time, you'd better listen to me."

I plunged toward a pair of my sweatpants, stubbing each big toe. I quickly flew into them and shoved my throbbing feet into snowmobile boots as I blundered out the door, grabbing a flashlight in one hand and a dog leash to use as a lead rope in the other.

Ren strutted toward me, full of an energy I'd never seen before. His neck was proudly arched, and his eyes were afire in the moonlight. But he obediently followed me through the yard, through the gate, and back into his pasture. Once he was securely confined again, I walked through the pasture and shone the flashlight all along the fence, searching for the obvious break. Ren followed, almost tiptoeing along behind me. Every time I turned around to see where he was, he stopped, but he was always just shy of ten feet of my backside. I could almost hear him shushing himself so that he wouldn't laugh too loudly and let the secret be known.

In the far back corner of the pasture I found one bent post. And, sure enough, there were frying-pan-sized hoofprints just on the other side of the fence at that exact spot where the post stood feebly leaning toward the hayfield. That cliché about the grass always being greener on the other side isn't merely someone's catchy phrase. It's a horse's motto, and each one seeks to bring it to fruition on a daily basis—and when their owners least expect it. Ren had obviously leaned across the fence to sample the exact same forage that was growing in his pasture. He'd accidentally bent the post and then simply stepped over the electric tape, finding himself totally loose in the field.

"You stay home, fella," I said to Ren, shaking my finger at him. I could have sworn that he had a grin on his face as I gracelessly pitched myself over the tape fence, flinging both boots off in the process. Each one flew off in a different direction; I could find only one. Ren turned around and headed back to the shed with a toss of his mane.

It was easy to retrace the steps of his excursion; the hay was flattened over all along the path he'd made as he strolled along grazing freely, just as his wild ancestors had done.

A queasy feeling rolled around in my stomach as the hoofprints turned away from the hayfield and headed directly toward the road. At three in the morning, in the remnants of the ninety-degree heat from the previous day, wearing a flimsy T-shirt stuffed into sweatpants and with one snowmobile boot now on one aching foot, I stumbled along on painful toes in hot pursuit. I was such a pretty sight. If a police officer had happened to pass by, he'd have surely wanted to know what I was up to. Ren had chosen to come back home by way of the road. Thankfully, he had stridden along the fence line and hadn't ventured into the road itself or across it—at least that's the story the hoofprints told. Then he'd turned into the driveway and walked in as straight a line as John Wayne might be capable of, right up to the house. He had rummaged around in the bushes right under the living room window, moseyed along the front of the house and to the side, and come to a nice square halt right where I had found him—where *Callie* had found him.

After I'd pushed the damaged fence post back in line and double-checked that the electric fence was surging, I went back in the house and back to bed. It would be time to do chores all too soon. Callie joined me on the bed, flipped my hand, and motioned for a tummy rub. George, in his best basset form, had calmly assessed that there had been no good reason for getting up and had continued to sleep. He was snoring when I returned to bed. I lay awake for a while, pondering all of the things that *could* have happened. Ren could have eaten enough rich hay to make himself sick. He could have wandered into the road and killed someone when they hit him or swerved to miss him. He could have sashayed onto a neighbor's property and discovered that their car or the siding on their house made a good scratching post, leaving behind his signature, elephant-sized dents. He could have just kept going and not have returned home. Part of me sensed that he knew exactly what he was doing and that he'd planned every step. He'd done the forbidden and taken a risk all on his own and could now go to sleep with a great feeling of accomplishment. Perhaps, when we all face our twilight years, we are teased with the steady ticking of some little internal clock, reminding us of promises we've made to ourselves.

"Just once, before I go, I want to sky dive."

"Just once, before I go, I want to climb a mountain."

"Just once, before I go, I want to write a song."

Ren never challenged the fence again and never appeared to show any more interest in the hayfield after that night. From that first day when I met Ren standing in the pasture with that single strand of wire level with his knees, to the many times I confined him in portable fencing, he always knew he was supposed to stay in whatever type of enclosure corralled him. He'd always complied with the rules—except for that one night.

Ren completely submersed himself in his new home. He was busy every day inspecting things, watching the deer in his hayfield, patrolling his pasture. He always found something to nibble on or something of interest to entertain him. He knew where every rock and discarded elm branch was in the back pasture. He also loved the front pasture and would stand near the road and watch traffic pass. In that front pasture, a slim solitary maple had taken up residency. I had been planning to dig it up and transplant it, since some maples are poisonous to horses. But Ren found it before I had the chance. The other horses had also discovered the tree, but they had no interest in it and left it alone. Ren was always in search of a good scratching post, whether it was the old mobile home on Joe's farm or a telephone pole. He was a creative opportunist. I watched him from a front window the day that he took a gander at that little maple. I could almost hear the cogs turning in his noggin as he approached the tree and then stopped, contemplating his next move. He began by scratching his chin on the slender tree. But the tender branches only bent away from his pressure. So, in order to create some resistance, Ren kept walking forward, trying to rub his head on the branches. He walked right over the top of the tree. The poor little thing was bent under him, trying to stand while it rubbed the full length of his body. Once Ren had walked over the tree, dragging it along his belly, it sprang up behind him with a wobbly "thwang." Ren immediately turned around and, with coltish playfulness, straddled the tree again and walked the length of it until it popped up behind him. Then he did it again, and again, and again, just like a little boy having a blast playing in water gushing from an open fire hydrant. Such forbidden delights don't happen that often, and you just can't pass them up, even though your mom would have a conniption fit if she knew. Each time Ren passed over his new belly scratcher, the maple became a little more lopsided and lost another handful of leaves. I briefly toyed with the thought of going out into the yard and shooing him away from the tree, but he was having so much fun. Besides, I knew I'd never get out there in time to rescue the sapling. I also thought of all the years that Ren had had no recourse and no relief from the headache because of his teeth. It just didn't seem fair to deny him the pleasure of getting at his itchy belly. When it was all over, the maple was thoroughly mangled. All that remained were a few splintered toothpick-like sticks protruding from the soil. The leaves had been pulverized into confetti.

Later that week, I bought a wooden back scratcher at the dollar store. Instead of using it on my own back, I placed it against Ren's belly and began vigorously scratching him with it to get those itchy spots for him. When my hands got tired and I had to stop, Ren followed me, sometimes cornering me so that I couldn't get away from him. He'd shove his muzzle at my hands and fling them up and apart, trying to make them work again. Sometimes I would give in and oblige with another session. I tried the belly scratcher on the other three too. Once they learned how good it felt, all four horses would line up as if pleading, "Do me! Do me!"

The first summer was beautiful and like a fairy tale come true. The days were sunny and golden and the nights filled with stars and sweet, outdoor smells. When it rained, the hayfield smelled even sweeter. Sometime between midnight and the first blush of dawn on one night near the end of summer, I couldn't sleep. I got up to get a drink of water and looked out the kitchen window. There was a silvery full moon casting its luminescence artistically onto the earth. Ren was up and standing right in line with the back door. There were no other horses up. They were asleep in the barn. My breath almost seemed to be snatched by the moon and carried away when I saw Ren standing in the translucent light. His mane almost glowed, and his big body stood out as a majestic silhouette against the stars. I wanted to freeze the picture forever and etch it into my mind so that I might not ever forget it. I searched inside the refrigerator for an apple or a carrot, but I was out of both, so I dug into an abandoned box in the cupboard and grabbed one little treat that I thought he might like instead.

I sneaked out of the house in my bare feet wearing just a nightgown and crept up to Ren. He always rumbled softly to me whenever he saw me. But, on that night, he didn't. He turned only his head to look at me, his ears sharply forward and his eyes focused on me. Something told me that Ren had known that I was coming out to see him long before I got out of bed. He'd been waiting for me. He also knew that, if he made noise, the other horses would awaken. So intent was the horse on keeping this our secret, that I almost expected to see him motion, "shh." I slipped through the fence and stepped into the pasture without making a sound. I opened my hand and looked down at the white lump, briefly studying it as I turned it over slowly with my fingers again and again. Such a small thing a sugar cube is. Seconds later, it was vacuumed off my palm and silently disappeared into a large equine mouth.

Ren's silken summer coat was cool to the touch in the night air, but underneath that heavy mane, his fur was snuggly warm. I buried my face in his mane and, with deep breaths, drank in the sweet pungent smell. I closed my eyes, nearly in a trance, and drifted in and out of my memories and pleasant thoughts. It was a mystical and deeply spiritual time to spend alone with a stately animal and a beloved friend. If either of us moved or made a sound, the other horses would stir and break the magic.

Ren knew the moon and the stars intimately. They were his companions of the night, and they had watched over him from the moment of his birth as a wobbly-legged colt. When the humans in Ren's life ended their day and went into their houses, Ren's life continued beneath the stars. We share the sun and the daylight with our horses, but seldom the eternal majesty of the night. I leaned my body against Ren's shoulder as we stood motionless, tenderly embraced by the endless canopy above us, and we breathed in the same night air.

So many of my dreams had come true, and, as I surveyed the beauty of my home, I felt complete. My life had been well traveled, over varied terrain, and had stood fast against the wind and storms that had frequently chased the sunshine away. I looked up at Ren, who was also limpidly gazing out into the stars that disappeared somewhere beyond the horizon. His dark eyes held diamond-like reflections of the moon as they blinked slowly and contemplatively; we were two best pals in quiet retrospection.

I've had a good run.

Ren probably would have stood with me as long as I remained at his side, but, in time, I had to go. I slid back through the fence and walked through the damp grass to the house. Once I reached the door, I turned back to look. Ren's face was turned toward me; he'd been watching and continued to do so until the door was shut behind me.

Goodnight, my friend.

CHAPTER
Thirteen

LIKE AN OLDER PERSON with arthritis, Ren found that his joints didn't move freely and strongly at the start of a new day. Mornings were difficult for him. Every morning after I'd creaked my own old bones out of bed, I'd stand at the south bedroom window and pause to prepare myself for what I might find when I opened the curtains. I'd pull them apart and keep my eyes closed for a few seconds and then slowly open them.

"Thank you, Lord, the Baby's up!" I'd exclaim the moment that I saw Ren up on all four feet, eagerly waiting for his meal.

Then Maali would whinny and let all of the others know, "She's up!" And the place on Townlane Road would come alive with the sounds and buzz of a real horse farm.

During the week, I was up every morning at six to do chores and get ready for work. On the weekends, I'd sometimes try to sleep in until seven. But it never worked out as planned. I could almost feel their big brown eyes boring through the walls and cornering me as I attempted to hide away and stay snuggled in bed for a few minutes longer. "Oh, all right," I'd mutter to myself and crawl out from under the covers. When I flung the curtains asunder, sure enough, they'd all be scrunched in the corner, looking sad and neglected. The moment they saw movement in the window, they'd all begin screaming.

On the weekends, I hitched Ren to the cart and we headed east down our road and then north on the next. Even though the roads are paved, traffic is minimal. We would venture only our time-tested mile out and mile back.

During one of our excursions, with my feet propped on the dashboard, I cheerfully sang Patsy Cline's "I Fall to Pieces" as Ren strolled along. He cocked an ear back and alerted me that a car was approaching from behind. With my extensive hearing loss, I relied on Ren to let me know if a vehicle that I couldn't see was near. Seconds later, an SUV whizzed past us at over eighty miles per hour. It was blur and had just barely managed to swerve in time to avoid hitting the cart and horse in its path. I shook my head in disgust and amazement.

"Tell you what, Ren," I said, "that's an accident on its way to happening."

I told Ren another story.

Years ago, when I was a trooper in uniform, I had to go to one of the auto plants in downtown Lansing. My mission was to deliver a "death message" as we called it. I would have to inform a man that his daughter had been killed in a car accident an hour ago. The man's supervisor had him awaiting my arrival in a private office. When I came through the door, a short, slim man rushed up to shake my hand. He had near iridescent twinkling blue eyes. His thick white hair was permed, and I wondered if his daughter had been the one who'd encouraged him to get the perm.

"I didn't do it," he said laughing. "I'm always happy to see someone from the State Police; the Big Law."

I had a few seconds to think of how innocent this man was. He'd probably never had a ticket in his life, and his view of law enforcement was almost child like and so free of negative influence that he felt completely at ease in joking with me. He'd gushed first, but then he read my face. My jaw was set and, although I shook his hand, I hadn't returned his smile.

Over the years, I'd delivered countless death messages. Sordid as it might seem, I was good at it. When there was a fatal accident, I would immediately turn my patrol car in the direction of the post to get the necessary information. I knew they would call me to deliver the message, and I *wanted* to be the one who knocked on that door. The message I carried would forever change that person's life, and the words I chose to deliver that message would be remembered forever. I was able to deliver the message each time with calmness and empathy.

The man stumbled over to a stool and slumped down like a forlorn, lost puppy. He looked up into my face, and waited for the words.

When I left the building and got back in my patrol car, I called in and told the desk sergeant that I was going to head out to some of the back roads and patrol along the cornfields. Just because I was good at it doesn't mean the emotion of it quickly slid away.

It was a sunny day in October. Leaves were changing, and farmers were harvesting corn. My radar screamed as it clocked an approaching vehicle at ninety-five miles per hour on a hilly, two lane road with countless side roads teaming with tractors and combines waiting to cross.

"Are you going to give me a ticket?" The nineteen-year-old driver asked with a quivering voice as her three friends listened and watched with wide eyes.

I should have written her a ticket. I wanted to scream at her. I wanted to take her car away forever. I wanted to haul her to her parents and tell them in person what she'd been doing. Instead, I told those kids every detail about my previous assignment. When I was finished, they were crying, and the driver promised that she would never speed again. I can only hope that the story stayed with her much longer than a ticket would have.

Ren cocked an ear back again to alert me about another vehicle approaching. A small, red car skimmed slowly along the side of the cart in the opposite lane heading north as we were. The driver was gawking, so I waved. Then the car pulled ahead of us and stopped on the shoulder of the road. A tall man wearing a baseball cap got out of the car and cautiously walked up to us. He had a sly grin on his face.

"This has to be the same horse," he said, starting to laugh. "And you're driving him now!"

The man must have read the perplexed look on my face and quickly asked, "Were you ever stopped with this horse in the middle of the road and some guy in a truck needed to get past you?"

The old blush, in all its flaming glory, spewed across my face as if it had been that day all over again. It was the same man who'd come upon me in his pickup when I was stopped in the middle of the road with Ren, and he wouldn't budge.

"Yeah, that was me," I chuckled, "That was *sooo* embarrassing."

"I'm glad to see you finally got him to move," he laughed.

"I don't know what got into him that day," I said demurely.

"Boy, he looks nice pulling this cart," the man said. "You're a long way from where I saw you before, many miles away. You didn't drive all this way, did you?"

"No," I said. "That place right down the road on Townlane with all the white vinyl fencing is mine. I bought it this year."

"That's a beautiful place," he said.

"Thank you," I said. Then I shook my head. "I can't believe you stumbled upon me again."

"It is strange indeed. I almost didn't believe it either; that's why I had to stop," the man said. "I kind of guessed your horse was pretty old back then, and that was several years ago. How old is he?"

"He turns thirty this year," I said.

"Isn't that awfully old for a horse?"

"Yep," I declared. "It's not that old for a saddle horse, but the draft horses just don't live this long. He's the equivalent of ninety in people years, and probably the oldest living draft horse in Michigan. Maybe even in the country."

"Amazing," the man said as he stroked Ren's shoulder. "He looks great. He doesn't look that old at all."

"He loves his food, even though he doesn't have many teeth left. He sort of gums his grain. And he's got arthritis, but we manage," I said.

"By the way, my name is Pete," the man said and we shook hands. "I have to tell you the rest of the story," he quipped with a familiar twinkle in his eye.

I smiled, leaned back against the bus seat, and set the lines down onto the dashboard, inviting him to go on. "So tell me," I said.

"The story of you and this big guy was one of the most hilarious things I've seen. Sorry, but that's the truth. I come around the corner in the middle of nowhere and here is this huge horse and this little person, almost placed there like props. You were talking up a storm to that horse; 'Come on, move!' You were clucking and whacking him with the rope, leaning your weight against him and pushing on him. All this big lug did was ignore you and sleep. The funniest part was, how did you get there? If you had walked there, how did the horse just stall, and why there of all places? It was like a scene in a sitcom. You can't imagine how that hit me. You had to see it from my perspective. After I talked to you and drove around the horse, I kept watching in the rearview mirror as you got smaller and smaller and smaller and *still* never moved. How long did you stay there?"

"I don't know," I said, laughing with tears in my eyes. But the tears were a mix of two ingredients that had begun to brew the moment I'd said that Ren was thirty years old. As those words had fallen from my mouth, they formally announced for the first time that there was a limit to the number of days ahead. But, at the same time, humor also tugged at my emotions, and won.

"He has a knack for these kinds of things," I said. "He has *experiences* I guess I'd call them. Sometimes they are very noble in purpose, and other times I just get dragged along like a secret serviceman trying to keep up with a runaway politician."

"It gets better," the man said. "I told this story to all of my buddies, and sometimes, when we're all together having a few beers, one of them will ask me to tell the story about the horse. I'm a storyteller, anyway, and of course I've embellished this one pretty good and set it in my home state of Tennessee. I always end the story telling them that you're still there to this day."

I was laughing appropriately, and Pete forged ahead.

"And it gets even better," he said. "One night when I was playing pool with the guys, my buddy Chad asked me to tell the story. As soon as I started, a pretty woman sitting at the table next to us said, 'What do you know about horses—you don't look like a horseman. What kind of horse was it?' Big, I told her. 'Not good enough,' she says, 'but finish your story.' I told her I'd finish it only if she came over and sat beside me. So she did. We've been married for two years now."

"Wow," I said. "What a story. No one would believe this ..."

"Yeah," Pete said, "and can you imagine what it's like running into this goofy horse again?"

"Now you've really got an ending to the tale. It's incredible that we met up again."

"As I was coming up behind you, I kept saying to myself, 'no, it can't be,'" Pete laughed. "I just had to stop and ask."

Pete said that he had to get back to work. We shook hands again, and Pete patted Ren on the forehead. "You keep movin' now, you hear?" he said as he shook the harness gingerly to reinforce his point.

"Good to see you again," Pete said. "I'm glad that you're moving."

Pete walked back to his car and hopped in. I sat for a few seconds, in awe of the whole scene, and then quickly picked up the lines. "We'll give him an ending, Ren," I said and tapped Ren on the rump. He sprang to life from his cat nap and jumped into an easy jog. I smiled a big toothy grin and waved at Pete as we sailed past him and continued north. The little red car never passed us. When we got to the next crossroad to turn around and head back home, it was gone from sight. I surmise that he watched us, once again, until we became smaller and smaller and smaller. But this time, we were the ones moving on down the road. And this time, he had turned around and gone another way. I had a feeling that he was gathering more ammo for his story. Some day, his kids will hear the story of the big, stalled Belgian.

Those were the happiest days of Ren's life. Every day was filled with his favorite things: sunshine, rain, food, and me. He loved to doze in the warm summer sun, but he loved to stand out in the rain even more. I've never known a horse that loved getting soaked as much as Ren did; whether it was rain or a bath, he loved being wet. When he was out in the big front pasture, he'd lazily graze, enjoying his world. His jaws made squeaking noises when he ate grass because he'd lost all of his molars by that time. The grass sounded like wet sneakers on a gym floor as it rubbed against his gums. Ren would graze for a while and then doze while standing by the fence right beside the road, just like an aged retiree sitting on the front porch watching the cars go by.

One morning, when I opened the curtains, Ren was not standing at the gate. My eyes were immediately swept from the gate to the back of the shed. Ren's stall had been broken through. The boards that were still attached hung in shattered pieces. I threw on some jeans and a sweatshirt and a pair of flip-flop sandals and raced for the pasture, calling Ren's name with every step.

Ren peeked around the corner of the back of the barn and came ambling over to me. I stroked his face. He had only a small scrape on his muzzle and minor scrapes on his back legs. That was the extent of his injuries. But what had happened?

Ren seemed disoriented and a bit confused, but he followed me over to his stall and watched with interest as I looked for clues. It appeared that he had been lying down, attempted to get to his feet, lost his balance, and then plunged head first right through the back of the barn. It didn't look like it would be difficult to fix, so I hauled my ladder, hammer, and nails down from the garage and out to the barn and commenced to repair the damaged stall. The boards had broken cleanly and popped back into place like pieces of a jigsaw puzzle. Just a few nails were needed to secure them back to the frame of the barn. Throughout this project, Ren was right beside me, ready to provide whatever supervision I might need. He stood next to me while I was balanced up on the ladder. Looking back, I realize that it probably wasn't such a bright idea to stand on a ladder next to a one-ton horse that had proven himself capable of knocking me off my own two feet. But it never occurred to me at the time that Ren would push on the ladder. He was content to watch, and found the whole event worthy of his full concentration. He'd drop his head to the ground, grab a stray leaf to munch on, and then lift his head back up to watch, like a person glancing down to grab just the right handful of popcorn from the bowl, and then immediately paying attention again to the movie. When I climbed down from the ladder and walked around to the front of the barn, Ren followed me and then followed me back to the ladder. He was as busy as I was, and I'm sure he felt quite important being included in the barn repairs.

When I was finished, Ren nuzzled me all over, messed up my hair, slobbered on both sleeves, got slime on my jeans, and snorted in my face. It ended up being a good day after all.

That weekend, I built a small addition to the main barn that was quickly dubbed the Ren House. All he needed was a standing-room-only place to get out of really inclement weather, if he chose, but not so much room that he could lie down. He went into his new little house to try it on for size and then returned to his pasture. He only went in the Ren House occasionally to escape the glaring, late summer sun or near torrential rainfalls. It was always his first choice to remain outside. But at least, with the addition, he could make his own choice.

On one gorgeous, sunny day, I was out in the outdoor arena riding Maali. Ren, Bonnie, and Prince were in the big front pasture grazing. A large, black pickup truck with a loud muffler pulled into the driveway. I didn't recognize the truck or the slender young man who slid out. He immediately walked to the other side of his truck and fumbled with something I couldn't quite see. Moments later, a little head full of blond hair also popped out of the truck. The young man held one of the most beautiful little girls I've ever seen. She was perched on her daddy's arms, almost on his shoulders, as he walked toward the arena fence. I dismounted Maali and began leading her toward them. The man was probably not much more than twenty-one. He was wearing a grease-stained mechanic's uniform and a huge, friendly smile.

"Hi, my name's Mark," he said. "I was wondering if my daughter could pet your horse."

"Sure," I said, extending my hand to Mark. "What's her name?"

"This is Katie," Mark said tenderly. His eyes fell down onto her golden, wavy hair for a few seconds that conveyed, *and she is the center of my universe.*

"She's crazy about horses," he said. "Every day, when we pass by, she says, 'horses' and points, and laughs and gets all excited. I've been telling her that, whenever we see someone, we'll stop and she might get to pet them."

"How old is she?" I asked.

"She's not quite two yet. There are times she's asleep in the truck, and I think, *Okay, I can just sneak on by.* But it's like she's got some little alert system in her that tells her to wake up just in time to see the horses."

"Sounds like you're going to be buying a horse someday," I said with a wisp of a smile.

"The neighbor has horses and we can't keep her out of the pasture; she'd crawl over there to get to them if she could."

"You've never had horses?" I asked.

"No, she started this all on her own. My wife and I don't know where it comes from."

"I do," I said wistfully. "This is something she's born with and it will never, ever go away. One day you're going to *have* to get her a horse, or, quite frankly, she'll make herself sick because of this love."

"I don't doubt it," Mark said. "Someday, maybe someday we can get her a horse of her own."

"It isn't 'maybe,'" I said. "You'll have to get her a horse. I know. I was the same way."

Mark smiled and pressed Katie closer to him. He gave her a kiss on the cheek.

"Having a horse is also great for kids because it keeps them busy with other things besides drugs, alcohol, and everything else that grows them up too fast," I offered.

When I was in my early twenties, my dad asked me to give him a photo of Mc-Keever, another horse I had owned. He didn't say why he wanted it, but I found a photo and mailed it to him. Several months later, the mailman delivered a box to my door. In it was a piece of wood from a pine tree stump. It had been cut, sanded, and smoothed to perfection. The photo of Mc-Keever was mounted in the center, and the whole thing was varnished and shiny. On the back, my father had written: "To Mc-Keever, thanks for taking care of her." He'd simply signed it, "Dad" on the front. A year later, he was gone. Since I'd grown up in a large city, drugs, alcohol, and sex were readily available at the schools I attended. But the horses had pushed every one of those temptations aside.

Katie's eyes were glued on Maali, and, when the horse reached her muzzle across the fence toward the little hand, Katie giggled the moment she touched the mare's soft nose.

"Would Katie like to ride?" I asked.

Mark's smile filled his face. "Oh, would she!" he said, and quickly brought his daughter through the gate. He lifted Katie up onto the saddle as I stood quietly petting the mare. Maali instantly knew that she had been loaded with precious cargo and stood statue still as we got Katie situated. When the pint-sized equestrienne looked secure, I started to lead Maali around the arena. Her daddy held onto her tightly so she wouldn't fall. I expected to look up at Katie and see her grinning and looking down at Maali. Instead her cherubic face was aimed over her shoulder as she studied something else.

My eyes followed the direct line from Katie's eyes to where they were riveted.

It was Ren.

Minus all heraldry as usual, the horse had quietly come over to stand with his head hung over the fence, to be as close to us as he could possibly get.

"That's the one she loves the most," Mark said. "He's usually standing in that corner right by the road, and, every time she sees him, she says, 'my horse.' She thinks it's her horse."

Katie's horse was now the closest she'd ever been to him, and there was nothing else that existed in her world at that moment.

Without speaking, Mark lifted his daughter from the saddle, and I stripped the tack from Maali and let her loose in the arena where she promptly rolled in the sand. Held tightly in her father's arms, Katie began clapping her hands together the closer she got to Ren. But she could no longer contain her all-consuming joy and, much too soon, lunged for the horse with her arms fully outstretched. Had Ren's face not been there to catch her, she would have vaulted over a four-foot-high fence and plunged from Mark's arms straight to the ground headfirst. But she latched her arms around Ren's face, and Mark held her frantically by the mere hem of her pant legs. Mark reeled Katie back into his arms and held her close. Then Ren moved one step closer so that the child could still reach him. Katie put one tiny hand on each side of Ren's large face and just pressed them together. She had not yet learned the stroking or petting movement; all she knew was that she had to have her hands on that horse in any way that she could. Katie squeezed her flattened palms tightly against Ren's face and giggled. She never once looked at her father or me, only down at her hands and what they finally held.

Most horses would have panicked at anything rushing toward their head and reared back. But Ren's savvy resolve had held him firmly in place as the child had leaped toward him. Katie would have stayed with Ren all day.

"We'd better let this lady get back to work, Katie," Mark finally said. "Can we come back sometime?" he asked.

"Stop any time," I said.

Katie let go of her horse and put her arms around Mark's neck. As Mark walked to his truck, Katie swiveled around so that she could keep her eyes on Ren. All throughout the time it took for Mark to go to the passenger side of the truck, get her buckled into her car seat, and then jump up in the truck and strap himself in, Katie's eyes remained fixed. As Mark backed out of the driveway and the truck headed east, I could barely see the little blonde head through the truck window. She would watch Ren until he disappeared.

And so it begins again.

One day, Katie will be able to speak of her love for horses and her need to be in their world. Perhaps her daddy will tell her how he carried her in his arms to see a big red draft horse and how the horse had caught her when she lunged for him. One day, her passion will have voice and, somehow, some way, she will find her way to a horse. But until then, only the angels know.

Ren had a spectacular summer. We had visitors. We had sun and rain. We had peaceful drives in the cart. Every day, when I came home from work, he had a refreshing bath in the hot sun. He still had struggles getting to his feet, but, once he was up, he was happy. I knew he felt good. He *patrolled* his pasture. He strutted all around, frequently breaking into a trot for no apparent reason other than he simply felt good. And that summer, he did his pasture patrol with an added feature. He was thirty years old, a gelding no less, and there he was, cavorting around the pasture like a colt—with a full erection. It's doubtful that Ren had ever been used as a stud before, and he never showed any interest in the mares when they were in heat, so it wasn't necessarily biology that convinced him to do this. I don't know what it was. When I told a few of my men friends about this, every one of them smiled and chuckled softly. They cheered for Ren. "Makes us older guys feel good," Ken said, as he tried to explain what a woman cannot understand. "Like there's hope for all of us when that old coot can do it," he finished.

Hmm.

One day, as I took a wheelbarrow of manure out to the pile, I saw part of the woven fence smashed. It looked like a gigantic boulder had squashed it. I walked over to more closely examine it. I looked at the fence and glanced at Ren, who was in the process of dumping over the wheelbarrow. Obviously, he had sat on the fence. In his efforts to get up, he must have fallen backwards and landed on it. Yet, he'd somehow managed to get to his feet without a scrape. The fence, however, was flattened.

As well as Ren had been doing, it was so easy to forget his age and dismiss reality. Then we'd have an "episode" and the truth would come crashing in all around me again. When Ren was on his feet, the quality of his life was superb. He also looked fabulous. There was no reason to take his life from him. Yet, common sense hovered overhead, and the inevitable cast a creeping shadow, like clouds that catch up and pass over you as a storm is approaching. What if Ren toppled through the fence and got out on the road? What if he got down in the night and became seriously injured as he thrashed around? These were questions that I tried to keep at bay, but they kept bouncing back. I wanted to see only how much Ren was enjoying life. I didn't want to deal with the ramifications of the episodes.

Sometimes I found a new chip gouged out of the barn or a new bend in a fence post. There were steady and increasing reminders. And then, one day, there were no more obvious signs of his difficulties.

I knew that Ren's back legs were permanently impaired, and I knew he hadn't given up on going "down." So I couldn't figure out why there were no other signs of struggle. But perhaps during one early morning challenge, resourceful Ren had devised a new way of getting up. By the time I saw what he was doing, he'd long perfected the technique. He was down snoozing, and, when he decided it was time to get up, he positioned his hind legs under his body as a horse always does to rise. But he lurched himself ahead, using the bulk of his weight to thrust himself forward onto his front legs *first* for just a few moments, and then he made one final, heavy push and got his back legs under him and his weight supported. He stood rock still for just seconds, like a weightlifter does immediately after jerking the bar to his chest, getting his feet under him and pushing off to stand completely upright only when the load was balanced. As soon as Ren felt his weight stable, there was one final thrust, and his body was supported by all four feet. Once again, he paused, as if to make sure the load would hold before he took a step, and then he walked off as if there had been no difficulty whatsoever.

As summer was rounding the corner and the days began to get just short enough to notice, it was in the back of my head that this had been Ren's last summer.

He had made it a good one.

CHAPTER
Fourteen

AT THE CLOSE OF summer, there is always one solitary leaf that is the first to flutter down. But you never notice that first leaf. Then another leaf drops. And then another. Still, you barely notice, until there are bunches of leaves at your feet. Autumn comes, leaf by leaf, and will not be deterred.

In late September, there was another episode. Ren was down and struggling. On that day, his creative attempts didn't work. He tried valiantly to get those hind legs to push for him. But they wouldn't. He rested on the ground for a good fifteen minutes, panting, and then tried again. I was watching from the window. Over the last few years, both Ren and I had become somewhat desensitized to the challenges he faced every day. There was nothing either the horse or I could do, other than our best, to try to work through the problems when they occurred.

"Lord, get the Baby up," I said, trying my old, near magical request once again. When I opened my eyes, Ren was still sitting on his haunches.

When Ren heard me coming to him, he nickered—more to say hello and remind me that he needed a treat than to let me know he was in trouble. I dug deep into my pockets of Ren experiences and found one that I knew would work. I measured out grain for him, towed his black tub near him—but just out of reach—and stood back to watch. His eyes focused on the tub, and he fluttered his nostrils, softly nickering as if telling the tub he'd be there just as quick as he could. And he tried and tried to get to that tub, but every time he asked those hind legs to help him, they refused, and he collapsed again in a frustrated heap. Then he stopped. He stared at me. Ren wasn't staring to tell me to get his tub over to him. Our eyes met, almost as an embrace, in the exact moment that Ren realized something was very wrong. All those years had gone by, and no one had told Ren that he was a very old horse living each day on overtime. At that exact moment, I saw him pierced with the truth. I dragged his tub to a spot right beside him, and, as he began munching his grain, I trudged toward the house, carrying the weight of what felt like cement blocks in my stomach.

"This is it. This time, this is it," I whispered with conviction as I walked through the garage and into the house. I paused before looking out the window. But when I did and saw Ren still on the ground, I nodded steadfastly in agreement with my decision. He'd eaten his grain and was resting comfortably. I collapsed onto a kitchen chair, useless and stuck within my emotions.

Probably a half hour passed before some semblance of energy trickled back into me, and I was able to stand up and look out the window one more time. Tears filled my eyes to see him still down. His head was up and his legs were comfortably curled under him, but he was no longer trying. He'd given up. I wondered if Ren, just like Ruby, had made his own decision to stop living. I wondered if he had reached the point where he accepted that the end was near. There was a certain forlorn edge to the scene before me as a crisp breeze gently lifted Ren's mane. He looked so alone. When we are born, there are loving arms waiting to catch us and welcome us into life. But when we exit, we go it alone.

"Help me with this, Lord," I murmured.

And then I called Dr. Jansen. The receptionist said he could be there in two hours to put the horse down. My shaking fingers fumbled through the phone book in the Yellow Pages as I searched for excavators. I found one just down the road from my home.

"I need you to bury my horse," I said, nearly choking on the words.

There was a compassion-laden pause, and then the man said, "I can be there in an hour to see what you want me to do."

The last time I peeked, Ren had been resting. I would have to remain strong and focused to go through with the plans. Continually watching him would only make me sadder and hinder my ability to function. So, to help ease the pain of waiting, I numbly paced the floor in the living room instead. Callie and George paced every step with me—back and forth, back and forth.

A blue truck pulled into the drive. I took a deep breath and said out loud to George and Callie, "I guess this is it, guys." I stiffened my jaw and went out to meet Alex, the excavator.

"I didn't bring the backhoe yet; I wanted to come out and see what we needed to do first," he said as we shook hands. Then we walked around the side of the garage toward the pasture without saying anything further. Braced and calm, I refused to look at my horse.

"Is that the horse?" Alex blurted. "It doesn't look like anything is wrong with him; why do you want to kill him?"

My eyes flipped up and almost spun in their sockets like wild window shades to see the vacant spot where Ren had been lying. Then they shot like torpedoes in the direction of the elm tree. There was Ren, standing on all four feet and stuffing his favorite elm leaves into his mouth. My hand snatched at my mouth; I didn't know if I was going to throw up or explode. I babbled incoherently, and my eyes blinked like pistons firing away in an Indy 500 race car.

"He looks great to me," Alex said with a frown on his face.

At that point, Ren realized that he had a visitor. He tossed his head, whinnied and trotted over to where we were standing by the fence. Alex glared at me as if he had just met his first truly evil person.

"He's been down all afternoon; he couldn't get up; he's very, old," I stammered, tapering off into mere gasps realizing that nothing I said was making any sense. Surely it had appeared that I had opted for "the easy way out" and just wanted to put an old horse down that was no longer useful to me.

"Call me when you need me," Alex said firmly, as if to shake some sense into me. "You'd better call your vet and cancel with him." Then he excused himself and walked back to his truck. He was slightly rocking his head from side to side. Obviously, I was a very cruel, bad woman.

In a stupor, I somehow managed to traipse back to the house, pick up the phone, and cancel the appointment. But it was as if I were watching some peculiar alien performing the tasks for me. None of the events of that afternoon seemed real.

Overtime. Every single day was special. Ren had always had everything, but I indulged him in whatever I thought might make him happy and comfortable. He had several apples each day, and, if he wanted to stuff two apples into his mouth at a time and slobber me silly with applesauce, I let him. I kept him clipped like a show horse, and his mane and tail silky and glistening with shine spray even though fall was upon us and Ren had already grown his plush winter coat. Everything revolved around Ren. In truth, it probably always had. But the responsibility was much greater now. I couldn't go out of town or really go visit anyone *in* town for that matter. I had to keep close watch over him. He required special feed: oil in his grain, medicine crunched up, soaked hay cubes, and more oil mixed in with the cubes. He needed to be monitored closely.

He'd become a full-time horse. I was his staff.

CHAPTER
Fifteen

Aᴜᴛᴜᴍɴ ᴡᴀs ɪɴ ꜰᴜʟʟ swing. It was the first season change in our new home. All of the horses grew dense winter coats in preparation for Michigan's zealous and intimidating weather. The days got much shorter, and the heavens above seemed close enough to touch. Pendulous clouds waited, heavy with the nearing birth of winter.

There was less time in the daylight to do things with the horses. I didn't have electricity in the barn, so I fed them in the morning in the dark and again at night in the dark. The snow came prematurely that year, and then there was ice. It was no longer safe to ask Ren to pull the cart down the driveway and out onto the road. If I wanted to take the cart out, I'd have to drive in the hayfield where there was only fresh, fluffy snow.

I love the snow on my face and in my hair. I love the sound of it as it squeaks beneath my boots, and I love seeing it heavily decorate evergreens, like the richest of vanilla frosting on a cake. Ren loved the snow too. After a fresh snowfall, he'd tackle the deepest snow drifts in his pasture, and, like a massive plow, aim for a drift and power his way through it, sending arcs of white off to the sides. Sometimes, he'd turn around and plow right back through the same mound. It was a game, and no drift was too big or too deep for him to clobber.

There were times that winter that Ren stood in the far southeast corner of his pasture. He'd gaze out over his hayfield, with his ears up and alert. Many times I'd look out, hoping to see what had captivated

125

him so; perhaps it was a dog or a deer running across the snow. But there was never anything there.

"He seems preoccupied," I told Nancy.

"That's strange," she said.

I decided that he was probably keeping watch over the angels.

At the beginning of December, big, fluffy flakes came, the kind that linger for a while and make your head look polka dotted before they melt away. That first big-flaked snow makes you think of warm and festive things like apple pie baking, red ribbons, snuggly sweaters, and the scent of pine—Christmas. I can't imagine Christmas without snow.

In the dollar store one day during that first week in December, I noticed a display of battery-operated Christmas lights. Instantly, visions of an elderly draft horse with Christmas lights on his collar danced through my head. I bought two sets. And then I was on a roll. The dollar store also had Santa hats. I tried all of them on my own head and bought the largest one. A red-and-white-striped neck scarf completed the scene playing out in my mind.

In an isle of the Christmas decorations at Wal-Mart, I found sets of fake brass bells. There were five bells mounted on a strip of vinyl with a notched section at the top so that you could hang them on doorknobs—or harness hames. There were probably one hundred sets of these bells in a lower-level bin. I couldn't hang bells on my horse that had a tinny sound or a pitch that hurt one's ears. So, I proceeded to ring each set of bells. I'd bend over to the bin where they had been stacked, grab one, stand up and shake it. "Nope," I often said out loud and flung the defective bells back in the bin. Then I'd pick up another set, ring it, and toss it back. After ringing every single set of bells in the store, I found that none of them pleased me. I didn't find what I wanted. So I went to another dollar store. There, it only took four shakes to find exactly the bells I was in search of. They had a clear, pretty ring that lingered just enough after the bells were still. I bought two sets.

I took all of my new stuff out to Ren. He, of course, was mightily interested in the new gadgets I'd brought out to share with him. He wiggled his muzzle on the hat and scarf and seemed to enjoy the soft texture. He watched intently as I cut two holes in the Santa hat. I mounted it on his head, poked his ears through the holes, and then attached the hat with a bungee cord around his throat. He looked both adorable and hilarious, and the sight made me laugh out loud. The

Santa hat sat on his head a little tilted. It was long enough so that the pompon on the end bounced lightly and came to rest just above Ren's eye and slightly off to the side. I let him wear his hat all day long as he moseyed around the front pasture.

That evening, I led Ren up to the hitching post and harnessed him in the dark. He still had his hat on, and I tied his Christmas scarf around his neck. I draped his battery-operated lights all along his collar, and I hung each set of bells on the hames. The sky above was clear, and the full moon lit up the ground just enough so that we could see. I was bundled up and had a warm blanket over my lap as I drove Ren down the lane and out into our snow-covered hayfield.

The bells jingled sweetly with each shift of Ren's shoulders. He cocked his ears back now and then to listen to them too. Soft puffs of steam on each side of his face piped up and then evaporated as he breathed out into the cold night air. The pompon of Ren's hat flopped and bounced gaily. I sang my two favorite Christmas carols, "Silent Night" and "O Holy Night," and then only the first line or two of the others I remembered. No one was there to listen anyway, so it didn't matter if one line of each song got jumbled in with the next. It was my very own medley, and it suited us just fine.

The cart moved along slowly because Ren had to work much harder to tramp through the snow while pulling the cart, which had tires instead of runners, like a sleigh has. I had the sneaking suspicion that it was *supposed* to take more time. That small voice inside of me was telling me to pay attention and to fill my senses so that I might always remember. I closed my eyes frequently and listened to the silence of winter. The full production of the music of summer takes a hiatus and sleeps in the downtime of this season. You can hear yourself breathe. You can feel your heartbeat. And, sometimes, you can hear a slight wisp here and there as impatient little tempests of snow stir. We stayed out until almost ten. I wasn't cold, and Ren was happy. But one full trip around the field was enough for an old horse.

The next day, I went back to Wal-Mart. This time, I was in search of two flashlights that I could bungee or duct tape onto the traces of the cart so that I'd have headlights when I drove at night in the field.

"Where can I find flashlights?" I asked a clerk.

"Oh," a young woman said as she turned away from the Stove Top Stuffing she was stacking on a shelf. "You're the bell lady."

"The bell lady?" I asked, obviously dumbfounded.

"Weren't you in here the other night looking at the brass bells?"

"Yes," I said, recalling my visit to the store, but becoming even more confused.

"Me and a co-worker watched you. We thought it was so funn ... I mean, we just couldn't figure out why you stood there for so long and rang every bell we had. And then you left—without any bells."

I nearly split my sides with laughter as I envisioned it from the clerks' perspective.

"We didn't know if this was your idea of making music or if you just had nothing better to do." She giggled. "And, the funniest part was, after all that, you just walked away!"

I explained to her that I had been searching for bells to hang on my horse's collar, but that they needed to have a pretty sound. I told the young woman how old Ren was and how I'd come to own him, and I told her a few of his stories.

"That is so cool to do that with your horse! What a neat story," she said. "I've always loved horses, but never got to have one of my own. Sometimes I go to a riding stable in the summer. You should write a book about him."

I left the store with misty eyes. I enjoyed telling people about my horse, but I knew the day was coming when it would all come to an end and there would be no new stories to tell.

Savor it; make the most of it while you can.

There were a few days in December—after a melt and before the really heavy snow hit again—when I was able to take Ren down the road in his Christmas garb. It was so much fun; people passing by in their cars slowed down, pointed, and smiled. It was fun because it was a once-in-a-lifetime experience. I knew there would never be another winter with Ren.

Nancy and Tom came to visit one weekend close to Christmas so that we could exchange presents. They also wanted to go out in the cart. Nancy had been hearing me talk about how much fun it was to take the old horse out with all of his Christmas decorations. She could also hear the urgency in my voice when I suggested that they come up and go for a ride. So, that day we heaped extra clothing onto our bodies until we looked like life-sized floatation devices, and topped our heads off with goofy elf and Christmas hats. Then I hitched Ren, and we decorated him with his Santa hat, scarf, lights, and bells. The three of us sat side by side, laughing, shivering, and generally just being silly as the cart made one pass around the hayfield. All of that hoopla to get ready to go, and it took all of fifteen minutes for the actual ride. Then we were done. The temperature that day was ten degrees and, with the wind chill, registered a balmy minus twenty-two. It wasn't for another year that I learned how much Nancy and Tom do not like winter. They'd agreed to go on the freezing-cold cart ride only because it was important to me, and only because they, too, surmised that this was the last winter for my old horse.

My first Christmas in my new house was special. I put up and decorated a live tree, just as we'd always had when I was a kid. It was a short little thing, and the star on top was about level with my eyes. From that point, the portly spruce immediately broadened in fullness as it reached the base—a roly-poly Christmas tree. I placed the tree in my front window on the first day of December. Every night, when I'd come in from chores, I'd make chai tea, turn out all of the lights except the tree lights, and sit in the soft glow listening to Andy Williams sing "Ave Maria." It was a wonderful time. Christmas has always been my favorite holiday of the year. It almost seems like it's a separate season.

One day in mid December, as I was getting gas at a convenience store, a truck pulled into the next bay. It was towing a flatbed trailer with a backhoe securely strapped on top of it.

I quickly screwed the gas cap back onto my truck and hopped over the cement barrier that separated the bays.

"Excuse me," I said to the dark-haired man pumping gas. "Do you do excavation work?"

"Sure do," he said turning to face me. "Do you want some work done?"

"Not yet anyway. But I'm going to need to have a horse buried one day, probably sooner than later. Can you do that?"

"I can. When are you planning to do it?" The man asked.

"I don't know. He's old. He has a very hard time getting up, and one day he's not going to," I said. "But I can't say for sure when. Do you have a business card?"

The man reached beneath the two jackets he was wearing and pulled out a frayed card from a pocket. "I'm Charles Ritter," he said. "Call me whenever you need me."

I shook his hand and slipped the card into my wallet. Charles Ritter had a round, pleasant face with piercing black eyes. Immediately I sensed that he had a kind heart.

I knew that one day I would be calling him.

CHAPTER
Sixteen

IT HAD SNOWED THE night of December 22, and the fresh blanket of snow sparkled in the winter sun as if encrusted with tiny diamonds. I knew Ren would enjoy being out there, making the first and only hoofprints on a blank canvas. I had taken the day off work to stay home and write.

There is a window right in front of my worktable that looks out into the front pasture, so I could work at my computer and watch my horse as well. Callie and George lounged on the floor beside my desk. It was the start of a perfect day.

I got up to make some chai tea, slowly stirring it to savor the sweet, spicy aroma, and I carried the mug back to my office. When I looked out the window, Ren was sitting on his butt. I'll never know if he had tried to get down to roll in the fresh snow or if he had slipped and fallen, but he wasn't able to get up.

I dashed for the mudroom and my coat and boots.

With unerring tenacity, Ren tried to get those back legs to do something—*anything* that would help him. He tried and tried, then got tired and slumped back onto the snow completely spent.

I trudged through the snow drifts to get to the barn, poured some grain into his tub, hauled it back, and placed it close to him, but just out of reach. The more attempts that Ren made to get up, the more exhausted he became. Finally, he resigned himself to lying quietly in the snow. I brought out a blanket from the house and draped it over his back and shoulders so that he wouldn't get chilled. He made no further attempts to get to his feet. And then everything else just seemed to fall into place.

"I'll be there within an hour," Dr. Jansen said when I reached him on the phone.

"I can't get there until after dark, but I'll be there," Charles Ritter said.

Then I waited.

I went out every few minutes to check on Ren and make sure he was comfortable. He was content to lie on his belly and chest with his legs curled under him. His head was up and he was alert. I brought him an apple and hand-fed him the grain that was in the tub.

When Dr. Jansen's truck pulled into the driveway, he got out and immediately went to the back of his truck to gather his supplies. I knew he was measuring out the fatal doses. When he came through the gate toward me, the syringes were poking out of his chest pocket.

There would be no going back this time.

The first words out of Dr. Jansen's mouth were, "Let's try to get him up."

Surprised, and bolstered by a smidgen of hope, I scrambled to my feet and plowed through the snow again and back to the barn to get Ren's halter. Out of breath, I slid the blue-and-white halter onto Ren's head.

"Give me the lead rope," Dr. Jansen said. "Stand clear. Sometimes they thrash around or go over backwards."

Dr. Jansen stood directly in front of Ren. He wrapped the lead rope securely around both of his heavy gloves, and then he began to step back, pulling the rope tauter and tauter until he was leaning his full body weight back. Ren did begin to thrash, aimlessly at first, but he also sensed that the man was trying to help him. I could see the wheels turning in his head as he tried to figure out just how the mechanics of this worked, how he could best do his part. Ren pushed his back legs around and around and kicked against the snow. Dr. Jansen kept pulling, tightening whenever there was slack in the rope. Ren lurched forward, trying to throw himself onto his front legs. His shoulder and hip muscles quivered and shook violently from the intense strain, and then he suddenly collapsed onto his side, breathing heavily and breaking into a sweat.

Dr. Jansen stepped aside, gasping for air. He'd used every fragment of his strength to pull the horse to his feet. There was silence, punctuated only by the loud panting of horse and man.

"Are we going to put the horse down, Annette?" Dr. Jansen asked after a few minutes. "It looks like he's lost the use of his back legs."

I nodded. "I don't see any other way, do you?" I asked. "This is awful because, when he does get up, it's as if nothing happened."

"Is he eating good?" Dr. Jansen asked, still trying to catch his breath.

"He's only missed one meal in his life. He struts all over the pasture. We even went out in the cart yesterday," I said.

Dr. Jansen looked down at the horse, puffed his cheeks, and blew the air out. He looked at me and said softly, "One more try."

With the lead rope wrapped around his hands tightly once again, Dr. Jansen pulled back and down on the rope, groaning with the effort. He reefed on the rope, never permitting an inch of slack in the line as the horse leaned toward him. Sweat broke out on his forehead, and his arms were shaking from the strength he was exerting.

"Come on, get up! Get up!" Dr. Jansen growled at the horse through clenched teeth. He threw his head back over his shoulders demanding yet more power and then hissed again, "Get up! Get up, you! Get up!"

In one violent explosion of snow and horseflesh, Ren was on his feet.

Dr. Jansen released the pressure on the lead and staggered back. Both horse and man stood there glaring into the moment, fighting to fill their lungs.

They were panting. I was holding my breath. My mouth hung open. Hollywood could not create a man who would physically try so hard to help a horse. What I'd just witnessed had defied all logic and laws of physics. There was no way a one-hundred-and-ninety-pound man should have been able to pull a one-ton horse to its feet. But I had seen it with my own eyes. I will never forget it.

Ren whinnied at the other horses and began to pull on the lead rope. I don't think Dr. Jansen had any power left to continue to hold the horse. Ren was antsy, prancing in place and twisting and turning. I'd never seen him misbehave in that manner, but he wouldn't stand still. He whinnied, pawed, and fussed and kept looking toward the safety of his barn and his herd.

"Just let him go," I said.

Dr. Jansen opened his hand, and Ren whipped away the lead rope as he trotted full tilt toward the gate and down to the barn. He wanted no part of us. He knew we were up to no good.

Dr. Jansen shook his head. "They can certainly surprise us, can't they?" He chuckled. "He moves well. His legs are okay," he said as he watched the old horse literally fly through the snow, sending waves of it off to the sides.

I tried not to cry, but I could feel the tears welling up in my eyes; once again, that all-too-familiar rush of opposite emotions flooded in. It felt like little darts striking from different directions.

"How much bute are you giving him?" Dr. Jansen asked.

"One gram, twice a day," I said.

"Let's up it to three grams a day," he said. "That should help his arthritis, and the exercise is good for him. Keep him active."

"It's so hard to know when to do this," I said. "I've had to put horses down many times over the years, but this time it's tough. He's so darn happy when he's up. Look at him, he's gorgeous. No one believes he's thirty years old."

"Is *that* how old he is?" Dr. Jansen asked, turning to face me square on.

"Yes," I said.

Dr. Jansen shook his head in amazement once again. "He has to be the oldest living draft horse in Michigan. I've never known one to make it to that age," he said.

Dr. Jansen's eyes locked into mine. "The horse will tell you when it's time," he said.

We started to walk back toward the driveway when Dr. Jansen and I both stopped at the exact same moment and looked down. We instantly saw what had held Ren captive. There was a huge, smooth crater melted into the snow. Whether Ren had lain down or had fallen was of no consequence. But sitting on that big butt of his had caused the snow to melt enough so that he couldn't position himself to push off in any capacity with his hind legs. This time, his aged and failing legs weren't to blame.

Dr. Jansen and I were bent over at the waist, like little kids looking into a deep mud puddle. Still bent over, we looked at each other and started to chuckle.

"He was stuck in the snow," Dr. Jansen said.

We had a hearty, nervous laugh. But the humor was tainted with the harsh truth that we had come close to ending Ren's life. We would have found the crater, and realized the horrific mistake we'd made—*after* the body was towed away.

I canceled my appointment with Charles. I sat in the house for a while and talked to the Lord. In truth, I couldn't talk. I just sat in a big confused lump for about an hour. But, from that day on, I started thanking the Lord for each and every day I had Ren. Every morning, when I parted the curtains and saw the big red horse standing by the gate, I'd say, "Thank you for one more day."

I still hitched Ren to the cart once or twice during the week and navigated my chariot and great steed around the hayfield. The going was slow through the ever-increasing deep snow, but it was obvious how much Ren loved it. His ears were always up and his eyes alert. Sometimes he'd try to prance in the deep stuff, and I'd have to tell him, "Easy, easy," for fear that there could be ice beneath the snow and he could slip and fall.

There is an awkward phase in a relationship when you get that unsettling feeling that it's coming to an end. It's like reading a good book, and you know you have only one or two more chapters left, and you don't want to read them because that will be the end of the story. Or, it's like visiting another state or even another country where you meet someone that you spend time with. You know that, at the end of the seven-day period, or whenever the vacation comes to an end, you are going to fly back to your home, never to see each other again. As that final day approaches, you nonchalantly, yet earnestly, try to cram as much living into those final hours as you possibly can. That winter with Ren, I was so much more aware of what little, yet unknown, amount of time we had left. I didn't want it to end. I wanted to believe that, if I kept spending time with him, I could prove that he was busy and still had more to do with his life. But I knew that time was running out.

When the temperature hit zero and the wind chill was much lower, the horses all had blankets to wear. I found a huge blanket trimmed in kelly green and navy blue that fit Ren pretty well. It was snug in the shoulders, but it would keep the wicked west wind from biting into him. He'd never had a blanket on in his life, and, when I first put it on him and strapped him in, he took off at a trot all around his pasture. He rolled his tail over his back just like my Arabians do, and he snorted and pranced like a yearling. I had to laugh; wouldn't I do the same if someone handed me a brand new winter coat?

One day, I looked out to see that Ren was in the pasture prancing and dancing like a crazy horse, turning around, walking short distances, and prancing again. I could tell from the window that he was snorting. His head was low to the ground. *Now what's he up to*, I thought, and went to the cupboard to get my binoculars. Enough time had lapsed that he was used to his blanket, so that wasn't what had him so excited.

It was a bunny.

One brave, little rabbit had ventured into Ren's pasture, perhaps in search of some tidbits of hay or dropped grain, and had come face-to-face with the big guy himself. I winced, thinking of one huge hoof stepping on the little thing. *At least it would be a quick death*, I reasoned—because the poor bitsy creature would be instantly flattened. But they were playing. The rabbit's smooth and luxurious coat and his round pudgy body all spoke of his youth. This was probably his first winter. The tiny fur ball could have scampered out of the pasture and to the safety of the hayfield, but he stayed in the game. The bunny would hop in circles and Ren would follow, with his big nose to the ground, trying to touch the small creature. Then Ren would get excited and prance away a few steps and come charging, high stepping toward the bunny as if to stomp him. But he'd stop just short of squashing him. The rabbit would dash around in its little circles, and the game would continue. I watched until the rabbit stopped and sat crouched for a few minutes as if signaling "game over." Then he turned and dashed toward the elm tree and vanished into the snow and weeds. Ren followed him and stood on his side of the fence watching intently with his ears forward as if trying to coax his little friend back for one more round. He waited patiently for a good five minutes in hopes that the bunny would return, then he turned away from the tree and plodded over to his favorite spot by the gate. Ren never missed anything, and he made the most of every day.

One late Friday afternoon, I tied Ren to the hitching post that's beside the house and next to the driveway, and I began to give him a good brushing. A United Parcel Service truck pulled into the drive and a young man jumped out carrying a large box. I knew it was the container of horse vitamins I'd just ordered.

The man walked up to me and Ren with a clipboard in one hand and the box in the other. "Sign here," he said.

I put the brush down, wiped the horsehair from my hands onto my jacket, and reached for the pen. I noticed the man's face had suddenly crinkled into an odd frown. He looked down. I looked down.

"What?" I asked.

The man wrinkled his nose again as if that alone made a statement. I looked down again. I looked back at the man whose eyes now asked, "How could you *not* notice?"

"Oh that," I said as I finally saw the near-half-bushel-sized pile of poop Ren had just deposited at our feet. "You're not a horse person are you?" I asked.

The man shrugged. "I'm from Flint," he said, as if that might explain away anything.

I quickly signed the form and let the man return to the safe confines of his nice brown truck, and away he went down the driveway.

"Golfer," I said.

I gave Ren a pat on the rump. "Don't be embarrassed, Ren," I said.

I picked up the brush and began currying Ren's neck, leaving the pile to sit until I was finished grooming my horse.

"I've done some pretty embarrassing things myself," I told him. "Like the time I went into the drugstore and saw a glass bowl filled with gold, foil-wrapped chocolates. 'My favorite,' I told the druggist. 'I'll take a pound of those.' The druggist looked at me strangely. I wondered why he wasn't shoveling my candy into a bag. He glanced in the direction of the glass bowl, and so did I—twice. They weren't foil-wrapped chocolates, Ren, they were condoms," I said laughing out loud. "I never went back to that store."

It was almost dark when I put the brushes away and walked Ren back to the barn. I grabbed my "apple picker" on the way back, picked up the load and transported it to the manure pile.

During the next month, I noticed that Ren was spending increasingly more time lying down. He'd always enjoyed lying in the snow, but the frequency was increasing. He also began to shift the weight load on his back legs more. I surmised these changes were occurring because his arthritis and EPSM were bothering him. But he never became lame. Just like me, he probably had arthritis everywhere, so no one particular spot hurt or caused him to be gimpy more than any other. It made it difficult to assess changes, but the increased amount of time he spent lying down was strong evidence that Ren was declining.

There were times that I happened to catch him trying to get to his feet. I'd bundle myself up and go out to him with grain in his feed tub as incentive. I'd put his halter and a lead rope on him and use the same downward straight pull that Dr. Jansen had used to help him to his feet. It worked, not because of my strength, but because Ren had figured out his own way to help, although I never understood just what he did or how he did it. The minute he got to his feet, after hesitating to balance before standing straight up, he wanted that grain. Nancy and I often joked that Ren had mastered the art of *appearing* that he couldn't get to his feet in order to get those extra helpings of grain.

One night, on my way down to the barn to do evening chores, I couldn't see Ren. I found him behind the barn, sitting on his butt, dangerously close to the fence. He'd been trying to get up and had managed to scoot himself closer and closer to the fence with each attempt. This was not a good situation. In his struggles, if he fell over backward, he could become badly injured and very frightened. I tried and tried pulling on the lead rope, giving him something to brace against. But he couldn't do it. I went into my tack stall and got my driving whip. When I returned to him, I began tapping him on the haunches. Well-trained horse that he was, he knew that this meant he was supposed to go forward. I kept tapping, a little more forcefully with each gesture.

"You gotta get up, Ren. Come on, get up!" I shouted sternly, and I kept applying the whip.

I gave him one final, hard crack. It worked. With one shuddering heave of his body, Ren jerked himself up and stood. He didn't go over to the grain immediately as he always did. Instead, he remained in one spot to catch his breath. I brought the feed tub over to him. I had never had to bring the feed tub to him once he was standing.

I went into the house and heated up some soup. But I could only stare at it.

Not once in my life had I ever struck a horse with a whip.

CHAPTER
Seventeen

In March, the time that Ren spent lying down was still increasing. Sometimes he needed assistance rising, but, most of the time, he was able to manage for himself. It was a constant worry that he might get too close to the fence again, smash into it, and get hurt or get loose. I was also becoming more concerned about Ren being down in the night in the cold and not being able to get up for the entire night. It's not good for any horse to lie down for extended periods because their bodies are so large and their legs need to support weight to ensure good circulation. To be down for an entire night would definitely not be good for an old, arthritic horse. And, since Ren loved being outside so much, whenever he did lie down, it was on the cold, hard earth. Even though he had a stall of his own with deep sawdust for bedding, he loved the outdoors so much that he seldom went in it. He preferred to stand at his post by the gate or out near the hayfield in his favorite corner, talking to the angels. If a young horse lies on the cold ground, it isn't a problem because it can quickly jump up at any moment. But it would not be good for Ren.

On the fifth of March, in the evening, I looked out the window to see Ren lying right beside the fence in the exact spot where he had stood on that summer evening when I had gone out to share those magical moments with him in the moonlight. It was eleven o'clock and bitterly cold with our usual west wind. I went out to him.

Ren's front legs were stretched out in front of him this time. I'd never seen that before. They should have been curled beneath him—the normal position he would assume in preparation to stand. I tousled his forelock and thought that, if he was lying quietly and appeared to want to lie down, I shouldn't try to force him to get up. I started to return to the house. Ren made a very soft nicker.

Don't go.

I turned back and shown my flashlight around the area where Ren was lying. There were flattened areas of snow all around him, proof that he had been struggling more than I'd ever seen. This time, the snow was only about two inches deep, so he wasn't stuck.

Once again, we went through our routine of me pulling with my full body weight against him to keep the rope taut and Ren doing his part. He managed to get to his feet, but there was no great thrust to propel himself forward and up. He more or less eased up onto his feet, staggered a few steps, and then had himself balanced enough to walk forward. I gave him a pat on the neck and went into the house. But I sensed that, this time, it was all very different, and it felt as if there was a heavy fog that hung over my head and then permeated into my soul.

At one o'clock in the morning, I woke up. Ren was down again in the exact same spot right by the fence. He was trying to get to his feet. Tears began to spill down my cheeks. The loneliness of the scene was blunt and heart wrenching.

Once again, we fought together to get him to his feet. This time, once he was standing, I left his halter on.

Back in the warm house, I sat at the kitchen table in my coat, knit cap, and gloves. "Help me through this, Lord," I prayed silently. "Guide me. Tell me what to do."

I looked outside. It had only been an hour. Ren was down again and was once again trying to get to his feet.

From that point on, I was out in the pasture every hour helping him. Ren was clearly in distress. It hurt him to stand, and it hurt him to lie down. He couldn't get comfortable no matter how he positioned himself. But still, we worked as the team we'd always been. Each break in between, I went into the house and sat, not bothering to remove any of my heavy clothing. At five, when Ren was standing, I sat on my bed, leaned back, and fell asleep.

I awoke at seven when the dogs alerted me that it was time to let them out. I was exhausted and emotionally drained, and my stomach felt queasy as I stumbled over to the window. My shaking hands pulled the curtains apart. Ren was standing at the gate, waiting for his breakfast as always. I smiled, but my teeth started chattering as I remembered the ordeal from the night before.

Ren ate his breakfast, but he seemed preoccupied. He ate quickly, out of habit and need. There was a subtle detachment between us that made me feel cold.

Tired as I was, I went to work and forced myself through the morning. When I came home for lunch, Ren was lying down. It was sunny, and he wasn't thrashing around or sitting up. He was lying with his front legs curled beneath him and appeared content. But it wasn't good at all.

When I came home from work at the end of the day, Ren was down again. It was the first time that Ren had ever been down at meal time.

I changed my clothes and headed out to do chores. Ren was interested in the grain in his tub as usual. But he was sitting squarely on his butt with his hocks flexed and his feet awkwardly protruding up toward his belly. They were not even in a position to push off. All he was able to do was rotate half turns by moving his front legs around him, causing him to pivot on his butt. I put his grain tub right beside him. He looked down at it, but, since he'd never eaten while sitting on his butt, he wasn't quite sure what to do with it. He struggled and pivoted and then crashed in a heap until he righted himself, uselessly sitting again. He never even looked at the tub again.

Calmly and methodically, I finished all of my chores and made sure all of the horses were set for the entire night. I knew my focus would be elsewhere.

I went into the house and made three phone calls.

"Charles? Can you come out tonight to bury the horse?"

"I can be there in an hour," he said.

The next call was to Dr. Jansen's office. It was after five o'clock, and the office closed at five. But the receptionist said that one of the doctors was still in. She put me on hold for a few minutes to see if the doctor would take one last farm visit.

"Dr. Jansen is gone, but Dr. Riley is leaving now," she said. "She'll be there within twenty minutes."

Then I called Nancy. I don't know what we talked about, probably the usual things people share at times like this.

"He had a great life," Nancy said. "You're doing the right thing."

"I know. I know," I said, "but ..."

"It's the right time; you just know when it's the right time," she said.

Strange how, at moments like this, you need a cheerleader rather than someone to merely share the trauma and sadness. Seasoned, life-long horse owners struggle with this decision every time we reach this point. It's never easy.

"Dr. Riley just pulled in," I said.

There was little conversation as I walked with Dr. Riley to the pasture.

"Is he still down?" She asked.

"Yes," I said. "He's never been down for supper."

When a horse is put down, whether it is lying down or standing, the process is swift and smooth. It happens within a matter of seconds. One shot is given intravenously to make the horse so sleepy that it slides down quickly to the ground. The veterinarian has barely enough time to remove the syringe. The second drug is administered immediately afterwards, and the animal has expired almost before the doctor has a chance to remove that syringe.

"That's it?" I asked, numb and stiff. "He's really gone?"

"Yes," Dr. Riley said softly as she let the stethoscope fall limply around her neck. "His heart has stopped."

Dr. Riley gave me a quick, sideways squeeze. There was nothing for her to say. She walked backed to her truck alone.

I stood beside my horse, oblivious to the wind and the cold. I watched Ren's sides, just to make sure. They were still.

Ren was gone.

I slumped down in the snow beside him. I stroked his blaze and buried my face into his mane and breathed deeply. I sat in the snow inanimately. But the memories swept over that barrier, like waves crashing over a pier. I remembered all the times that big white blaze was slimed with green; I remembered the joy in his eyes when he saw his cart for the first time and when he discovered the belly scratcher tree. I remembered the first day he wandered over to the fence to meet me and I touched that big muzzle. I remembered his John Wayne sideways-strutting and the puffs of dust from his footsteps as he strode toward me. I remembered his soft, low rumble, and I laughed, and I cried, and I did them both over and over. It was dark, and overhead the stars were beginning to sparkle against a velvet sky. I grabbed one of his big, old hooves and shook it. *How many miles,* I thought. *How many miles have they traveled?* He'd done the impossible. Ren lived to be thirty years old, an unheard of feat for a draft horse.

With my scissors, I cut off a huge swatch of Ren's mane and banded it at the top so that it wouldn't fall apart. I wound it around my hand and stuffed it into my coat pocket.

I led Maali and Bonnie up to Ren's body individually. Each stopped a few feet from him and didn't need to go any closer. They understood. Then I brought Prince out. Instantly, the leader's eyes shot down to his buddy, and he took two quick strides as if to get there swiftly to help him. He stopped and then looked away.

The stillness was sliced by the sound of a rugged motor as the backhoe came down my road. It was the only vehicle out there, and its approach seemed all the more processional because of its solitary presence. I looked up to see the headlights as they turned into my driveway, and I went over to open the gates. This was not an easy job for anyone; not for me, not for the veterinarian, and surely not for the excavator.

"Are you doing okay?" Charles asked.

I nodded.

"Where do you want the hole?" He asked.

I walked with him over to the far south-east corner of the pasture.

"This was his favorite spot," I said. "Dig it here."

We stood in awkward silence for several long seconds. I could hear myself breathe.

"There will be a large mound of dirt for a while," Charles said, breaking the silence. "But within a year or so it will all be flat again. You won't even know."

I nodded.

The quiet resumed. And then, panic seized me. "I didn't think about it," I said, "but are you going to be able to dig through the frozen ground?"

"Gonna try," Charles said. "Gotta break through the frost line."

We both turned to go; me to the house and Charles to his idling backhoe.

"Do you need me to be out here?" I asked.

"No, you go inside where it's warm. I'll be fine," Charles said.

I hesitated briefly and said, "I was thinking … in your excavation travels, if you ever find a large rock, like a boulder …"

"I'll see what I can do," Charles interrupted.

I pursed my lips and nodded securely and then walked to the house, leaving Charles alone in the dark to do the work.

I watched from the kitchen window. The black of the night was spotlighted by the headlights of the backhoe. I could hear the gears grinding. It was eerie, and I was shivering as I clutched my arms around my chest. I could no longer make out the large lump that was Ren. From my watching point, his body had become one with the darkness.

In order to break through the frozen turf, Charles had to ram the ground with the bucket of the backhoe—over and over. The concussion caused the window to rattle.

Boom.

Boom.

Boom.

The earth's resistance and the impressive noise seemed appropriate for the exit of such a great horse. It was a declaration.

I was here.

I mattered.

Charles was out in the cold, pounding away at the ground, for over two hours. The earth fought and resisted to open, but Charles never gave up. In time, I saw the bucket scooping and the backhoe pivoting to dump its load on the side. There was finally a hole in the ground. The rest of the job would go quickly.

Within a few moments, the huge piece of equipment turned to face the house and came steadily closer, toward Ren. The glare of the lights prevented me from seeing the horse's body. The machine paused for a few moments, and then the gears kicked in again and it backed away to the corner. I continued to watch, barely able to make out the outline of the backhoe as it pushed the dirt and frozen clumps into the hole.

At nine o'clock, the headlights of the backhoe bounced their way toward the house again. This time, the machine continued through the pasture gate and around the side of the house. The motor picked up speed as the vehicle hit the pavement. Soon, all sound of it was gone.

And the stillness of the night returned.

CHAPTER
Eighteen

THEN MORNING COMES.

On that first day after a loss, you lie in bed, or wherever you happened to collapse, trying to sort out dreams from reality. The truth acridly seeps in and sticks to you like pine pitch on your fingers.

I'd managed to sit on the edge of the bed and lean back. So all I had to do to begin the new day was sit up. My coat, hat, and boots were still in place. Still wound around my hand was the weighty mass of Ren's blond mane. It hadn't been a dream.

I wasn't quite sure what to do. Morning pays no respect to anyone, and she brings with her your individual measure of responsibilities. Callie alerted me with her little high-pitched yip that the horses were up and stirring. There were dogs to let out and feed and horses to grain. Somehow, you go about those first initial tasks because somebody has to do them and that somebody is probably you. But your actions are robot like.

In fragments, the activities that comprise your life and help to define routine quietly invite themselves back in, like brushing your teeth, walking to the mailbox to get the mail, or answering the phone. Such seemingly inconsequential tasks that, overnight, become conscious challenges, then become major accomplishments once you are able to complete them again.

No matter what ordeal you have gone through, the rest of the world doesn't stop. I remember how I was hit with that truth on the day my mother died. It was December 23. I had spent three full days in the hospital at her side, never leaving her once. When she was gone and I emerged from the hospital that had been my cocoon, I was instantly furious that the sun dared to shine on that day. I was even more furious when I passed several young interns walking into the hospital as I was leaving. They were laughing and talking about an upcoming Christmas party. How could they? We *want* the world to stop, acknowledge our sorrow, and pay respects. But it doesn't work that way.

Sometimes you are nagged by those inner thoughts that ask if you did enough, said enough, cared enough. Did you make the right choice? Could you have tried something else? Sometimes you might receive hints that you did everything correctly and, other times, the persistent questions just get pushed aside like worn out shoes in the back of a closet. Yet, either way, you have to press forward with your own life.

There is something so sweetly innocent and constant about the routine of chores and caring for horses. You awaken at the same time and head out to the barn wearing clothes that never match and sporting a good case of bed hair. It's the same every day. You measure out grain and hay, check water, and fill tanks. You might linger with each horse just long enough while its eating to scratch a favorite spot or spend a few quiet moments. And then it happens all over again in the evening. It doesn't matter what has happened in your day—what tragedies have occurred, what dilemmas you must solve, what decisions you have to make, or what places you have to go. The chores have to be done. You can take vacation days from your job or call in sick. You can decide not to go grocery shopping that day, you can turn your television off, and you can decide not to answer the phone. But you cannot decide not to do your chores. If you are late getting to those chores, you hear about it. There are times when you want everything that life contains to stop churning. But this is one part that cannot, and it's good that it doesn't.

Many years ago, I had an Arabian mare who died, leaving her four-day-old colt orphaned. It was crucial that I get him to nurse from a bottle soon, or he, too, would die. I had just lost my best broodmare, and I wanted time to stop so that I could grieve. Yet I had this new little life to care for. He didn't understand what had happened. He only wanted his mama, and he was hungry. The bottle I offered him was not the same as his warm, soft mother. But I had to find a way to make him nurse. In the wee hours of an exhausting and sad night, Little Joe began to nurse from the bottle. Pent-up tears gushed from me instantly. I cried in sadness for the loss of the mare, and I cried in joy because the foal was nursing. It was such an intense mix of emotions, the only way to describe it is that it was like placing your left foot in a bucket of ice water and your right foot in a bucket of boiling water. How does your brain sort out which one you are to feel the most?

When I got out of bed, I went to my window and paused. I knew Ren wouldn't be there. But until morning clears the vagueness of the night, we go through a brief phase where, in a strange way, you want to believe that your mom is still downstairs in the kitchen making breakfast, your husband is still outside puttering around in the garage, the old lab is still sleeping on the sofa. And we pause, with just a fraction of hope, before we summon the courage to make sure.

I pulled the curtains apart. Ren was not at the gate.

It was over.

CHAPTER
Nineteen

THE SHRILL, PIERCING CRY of a bird greeted me as I went out to do morning chores. It was May, and the grass was green and lush. I could smell the earth in the warm spring sun. These birds were noisy and boisterous and demanded recognition. My breath snagged when I saw two killdeers standing on the mound that covered my horse, and another swooping and diving overhead. They had selected and staked out that special spot to build their nests. I was instantly filled with warmth, as if a comforting blanket had been placed over me.

"My favorite birds," I whispered. "They came."

When the killdeers arrived, I took it as a subtle, sweet message that I had done okay as Ren's caretaker.

Things at my place had returned to normal. The chasm that Ren had carved into the previous five years of my life was empty; yet, it was slowly decreasing in depth. It was still Ren's home, and there were times I still expected to see him peeking around the corner of the barn.

Overnight, my chore routine had been abruptly changed. Everything took much less time. There was no more oil to spill and mix, there were no hay cubes to soak, and there were no broken boards or fences to mend. There was no need to remain fixed at home either. *What do I do with all of this time now?* It's strange how things filter in to fill in those gaps in your day. But they do, and that's the way it's supposed to be. New responsibilities come your way, and you even find other things to enjoy, one small pleasure at a time.

The horses shed their winter coats. The hayfield was cut and baled in June as usual. Life went on.

"I'm thinking of hanging Ren's collar on the wall," I said to Nancy one afternoon when haying was done. "I'd like to restore it, dye it shiny black again like it must have been many years ago. Maybe get some new brass toppers for the hames."

"That's a great idea!" she said. "You could make a mirror or a clock out of it." Then she added, "But what if you get another draft horse one day and you need that collar and harness?"

"I don't know if there will ever be another draft horse," I said. "Part of me thinks this was a once-in-a-lifetime deal for me. Not that I wouldn't have another draft, it's just that I don't think that it's going to happen. Maybe it's not supposed to."

Ren was a once-in-a-lifetime horse. I became increasingly aware of that every day as he pounded that truth into my brain with his massive hooves. And, as a glacier slowly yet forcefully changes the earth beneath it, Ren had changed my heart forever. There would *never* be another Ren.

I bought some leather dye and hung Ren's collar on the hitching post as I painted over it with the strong-smelling liquid. It dried to a satin finish in the sun. I hadn't lifted that old collar in many months, and the last time I had slung it over the hitching post, it had been in the winter with Ren standing there too, waiting to be hitched.

"He'd like to see this restored." I laughed to myself. "If Ren were here and could talk, he'd tell me that it was about time I fixed that up for him."

A few days later, I drove up to see an old friend of mine whom I hadn't seen in a long time. I was in search of two shiny brass toppers for the hames, and I knew he would have just what I was looking for.

"So the old horse is gone, eh?" Marvin asked.

"Yeah."

I'd advanced to the point where I could openly discuss his loss without much more than a hint of emotion.

"That's too bad," Marvin said. "He was a good horse. How old was he?"

"Thirty," I said simply.

Marvin put down the utility knife he'd been holding in his hand and stared at me. "I've never heard of one making it to that age," he said.

I just smiled.

"And now I want to hang his collar on the wall," I said. "You'd be proud of me; I dyed it black myself, just like a real harness maker, and smoothed some of the rougher spots out. It looks great and will be perfect with these brass toppers."

"Some of the English make clocks out of these old collars," Marvin said. "That's a nice way to hang it and get some use out of it."

I nodded in agreement.

Once I got home, I fitted the sparkling brass decorations onto the hames. They were perfect, and the collar looked complete and finished. I hung the collar on a heavy nail in the garage for the time being, thinking that one day I'd decide where to hang it in the house.

That evening, when I looked out the kitchen window, I noticed a large gray lump on the mound of dirt. I blinked quickly several times and swallowed hard. What the heck was out there? I grabbed my binoculars and peered out. I gasped and raced for my boots.

"He remembered ... he remembered!" I sang over and over as I headed out the door.

"It's perfect." I sighed in awe of its size and the obvious effort to get it there.

"Charles remembered my rock," I said. "And no killdeers got squished. It's all perfect."

The large gray-and-pink-toned rock surely weighed five hundred pounds. Now, I will always know where. It's there permanently for all the days that will ever matter to me.

Decades, perhaps centuries into the future, someone will come and dig up the ground to build something new, something needed. They will find the rock first, and then the bones.

I hear someone say, "Look at this. This must have been a special horse."

And the west wind will emit a soft, low rumble.

CHAPTER
Twenty

THE MEADOW WAS LUSH and green. The rolling hills all around me were dotted with dandelions. The sky was blue and clear, and the warm sun shone down on my shoulders as I stood there. I don't know how I got to this place or where I was. I'd never seen this pasture before. I could see myself holding a white bucket in my hand and slowly turning around, trying to ascertain my location. Suddenly, the earth began to tremble, and I watched myself look down at the ground, bewildered and afraid. Was it an earthquake? Then there was the sound of thunder approaching, getting louder and louder. But it was sunny. No storm was in sight. I couldn't walk, but instinctively turned in place to face the direction from where the thunder came.

Over the crest of a hill came a herd of horses. Waves of Belgians cascaded down the slope toward me. They galloped full speed, yet it all was in slow motion as they came nearer and then completely encircled me. There must have been one hundred of them. I was totally surrounded, engulfed by a sea of copper and bronze. Walls of surging muscles flexed powerfully, and granite hooves pounded so closely that they could have trampled me into the ground. Their blond manes rose and fell against the backdrop of red horse flesh. Their great hooves reached for the earth like precision machinery and hammered in, pulverizing it into nothingness, enclosing me in a cloud of dust. I was terrified and frozen in fear, trapped in the middle of tons upon tons of horses, and I had no possible means of escape. At any moment I, too, would be ground to powder. I reached out my hand toward a familiar long, golden white forelock, flowing to the beat of the gallop as it whipped past Ren's ears and down almost to the end of his muzzle. He tipped his head to me, but continued on.

I watched myself turn to watch them, thundering away toward the next hill, their massive haunches propelling them on as clods of dirt fired up behind them, showering the turf with shrapnel.

Then I awoke, gulping for air and shivering. It had been so real. For a few moments, I didn't know what had happened or where I was.

It had been a dream; yet, I had never come so close to thinking that I would be killed. At the same time, I was awed by the beauty of creation and the display of power that I'd experienced.

It had been too real. I could see them, hear them, taste the dust on my teeth. I could feel their hoof beats thundering in my chest.

Where is it said that our beloved animals don't go to heaven? Where is it said that their spirits don't go on? Christians believe that Jesus will return, and he does so riding a white horse. So then, where does the horse come from? If that's mere symbolism, then the entire Bible must be as well. The ideas of a God, creation, floods, parting of seas, and a virgin birth must then also be reduced to mere symbolism.

"Oh no, not *that* part," some would say.

Do we listen to what a particular person decides is truth and what is symbolism on a particular day? Are we supposed to carve up the Bible to suit our whim, to control, to instill fear? Even if animals do not have souls and are not worthy of heaven on their own, I believe in the power of my God and I believe in his love. When a beloved animal dies, I pray it up to heaven. I ask the Lord to take it there for me, and I believe the Lord answers that prayer simply because he loves me. But who *knows*, for sure, that animals don't go to heaven on their own goodness and innocence? We are promised a life after death where there are no tears. Would God send us to a place apart from the animals we loved? I refuse to believe so.

> *Do you give the horse his strength*
> *or clothe his neck with a flowing mane?*
> *Do you make him leap like a locust,*
> *striking terror with his proud snorting?*
> *He paws fiercely, rejoicing*
> *in his strength* ... (Job 39:19-21 NIV)

Such eloquence in God's word, and then we are supposed to believe that all that is left for the horse after death is to decay in the ground and become fertilizer for plant life? I refuse to believe so.

Life, as we know it, isn't meant to be forever. It's only a handful of moments compared to the eternity that we are promised. Once we reach that eternity, we are reunited with the loved ones who went on before us. Surely, in that new life there is a place where all of our poodles, calico cats, ponies, and bunnies are gathered to wait for us. There, endless acres of green pastures and rolling hills stretch into forever in a place where big Belgian horses gallop freely and without pain, their manes billowing in crystal clear breezes.

CHAPTER
Twenty-One

THIS MORNING WHEN I did chores and cut open a hay bale, a black object tumbled out—my missing snowmobile boot.

Now, here I am sitting in the kitchen with the old collar. I hauled it in from the garage after my morning chores, and plan to hang it tonight. I drew a dust cloth over the leather surface and touched it up with the black leather dye. The brass toppers are still shiny. I run my hands over that sandpaper-like, crusty horse sweat. When I'd restored the collar, I just couldn't make myself chip it off. Some of it was Ren's, and he'd earned the right to leave his mark there too.

It's the winter after Ren died. Christmas will be here soon. I've made popcorn, sprinkled with Parmesan cheese, and I've made hot cocoa—with milk. George and Callie think a popcorn night is the most wonderful thing of all, and they are waiting excitedly for me to toss them their share.

I'm remembering that crazy old horse—the mangled maple tree, the stalled sudden nap in the road, the John Wayne gait. I see him, once again, plow through the snow with his Santa hat bungeed to his head. No, I wouldn't have missed it for the world.

I laugh out loud imagining Ren in some great amphitheater striding slightly sideways up to the podium to give his honorary doctorate speech to the large crowd gathered there to hear him speak.

"He would love to wear a cap with a tassel," I say to George and Callie, who look up at me with their heads cocked, listening intently but hoping that more popcorn will miraculously fall to the floor.

"If he could only have talked," I say.

Prompted by a tantalizing idea, I chuckle and grab a pen and notepad. At the top of the page, I begin to scrawl, and the words tumble out onto the paper.

If Ren could talk, he'd say …
Eat every meal with gusto, and dream about the next.
Standing in the rain is good for your soul.
Learn to love the snow; it will always come.
Enjoy a good belly scratching.
When you are down, try with all your heart to get back on your feet.
Forget about what got you down to start with.
Learn the names of all of the stars, although it might take you thirty years.
Don't worry if your face is green sometimes and you look foolish. Her smile is worth it.
Don't dwell on what was.
Don't worry about what's to come.
There's never a good reason to pin your ears back.
Don't kick.
Don't bite.
Don't admonish without knowing all of the facts.
Be the first to say hello.
Life isn't just about you.
Be gentle with those who are smaller than you.
Go venture out into that hayfield one night and see for yourself what's out there.
Love beyond what your heart can reach, even if it's just for five years.

I read the list to George and Callie. "Life's lessons from a thirty-year-old draft horse," I tell them, nodding with approval. "He'd have lots to say."

I get up and pour another cup of cocoa, sit back on my kitchen chair, and listen to the clock faithfully ticking. Scenes from the morning after Ren's death revisit me, and I remember how, on that day, everything came together. After I'd done chores, I had intended to go over to the mound of dirt for a few minutes, just to see it. But my eyes were sharply drawn away as I glanced out into the pasture. Ren's hoofprints were everywhere in the snow: beneath me, to the left, to the right, in front of me and behind. Everywhere I looked, as I turned in small, slow circles and walked in all directions, his hoofprints were there. It was impossible to follow any of them. They covered the snow. I never made it over to the fresh pile of dirt.

It was on that day that the impact of Ren's existence hit me. He had managed to touch every area of my life, just as his hoofprints had covered every inch of that snowy pasture. He'd left his hoofprint in every chamber of my heart, every small recess in my brain. All I could do was stand out there in the snow and tremble as I tried to process the magnitude of one old horse's life and the messages it contained. And, even on that day, I was still being tenderly influenced. I had intended to go to the burial site, where death dwelled, but the hoofprints had drawn me away both physically and emotionally from becoming bogged down in grief that could linger far longer than needed. Immediately, I felt his presence everywhere. I could picture him standing under his elm tree. He was in the clouds above and in the stars that were beyond those clouds. I knew he would find his way into sunny days and into the raindrops that he loved so much. Whenever it snowed, I would remember him.

And so it is with death. The loved one who has left us is only gone completely if we choose to believe it's so. We might be attracted to physical attributes, but we fall in love with a sense of humor, a set of values, kindness, manner of expression, intelligence—the essence, the flavor of that life. We fall in love with all of the traits that we cannot touch. Perhaps this happens, in part, to prepare us for the time when the physical shell has been discarded so that we might listen for the subtle reminders of existence in another form.

Ren was just a horse. I suppose that there are those who would enjoy driving that point home and making it stick painfully like a dagger. Did Ren know that he had led such a colorful and meaningful life? I'd like to think so. But the truth is, he was just a horse. He couldn't talk, and he didn't have the ability to reason as humans do. He never earned a degree, never made a buck, and never traveled the world. He knew nothing of politics, recessions, and war. His needs were simple and basic. As far as he knew, apples just appeared before him.

Horsepower

Have horses resisted extinction because we still physically need them? We have vehicles and machines now that have taken their places. Other than to run races and compete in horse shows, why are they still here? If we are supposed to learn about being human only from humans, then why is the planet graced with dogs, turtles, cattle, and horses? Why so many forms of life?

Nothing is mere happenstance. There is a definite connectedness to everything that happens in the lives we forge as we walk this earth. We aren't in it alone. Sometimes we get to see how the pieces fit together and how they join, each piece having an impact on the one next to it, and sometimes we don't. It isn't just a wild game of chance or a lonely round of solitaire. All creatures have a purpose, and they cross our path for reasons. Perhaps our greatest teachers are the simplest creations.

I think about the totality of that horse's life—he was free of guile, deceit, jealousy, hate, and corruption. In the great scheme of things, Ren would choose to eat twigs; yet, his was a life that mattered. Perhaps that is but one more broad, sweeping lesson from an old horse—the importance of mattering and not letting one day merely drip into the next—doing something with the breath of life we are given, leaving behind some shred of evidence that we were here. And, maybe, the greatest form of mattering is never knowing that you truly achieved it. Then, some day, when those younger come to take your place, someone will sing a song for you ... someone will remember.

The horse wasn't given wisdom. He was given a flowing mane.

I toss George and Callie another handful of popcorn, sling the collar over my arm, and walk to the wall where I've pounded a sturdy spike into the stud. I hadn't lifted the collar in this fashion since the last time I'd harnessed Ren and placed it up and onto his shoulders. On that snowy day, I had been laughing with a beloved old friend.

The collar hangs on the wall at just about the same height it hung on the horse himself. In the linen closet, I reach for a certain brown paper bag on the top shelf where the Christmas decorations are stored. I take out a soft, red-and-white knitted mass and shake out the red Santa hat with the bouncing pompon and hang it on the tip of a brass hame topper. I don't back away for a good look, not yet anyway.

I pour my last dollop of cocoa and look out the window instead where the hayfield is sleeping, blanketed beneath wispy ruffles of snow. It's quiet except for the west wind that's always on its way. George and

Callie are asleep on the floor now, and the light of home is warm and peaceful.

In the sky, the stars are just beginning to assemble, and the cool violet of night is waiting to descend. With my hand on the light switch, I'm ready to turn and face the collar.

I nod firmly and smile.

It's perfect. The Santa hat sits a bit tilted. The pompon sits off to the side, unmoving. The brass toppers shimmer slightly in the soft glow of the Christmas tree lights. Yes, I have to admit—it would make a nice clock. But, it will remain empty.

It can't be filled.

9264678R0